Lectionary

Story Bible

YEAR A

Other Northstone and WoodLake titles
by Ralph Milton

Sermon Seasonings
God for Beginners
Is This Your Idea of a Good Time, God?
Man to Man
This United Church of Ours
The Family Story Bible
Angels in Red Suspenders
Julian's Cell
The Essence of Julian
The Spirituality of Grandparenting

Ralph Milton

Lectionary
Story Bible

YEAR A

Illustrated by Margaret Kyle

WoodLake

Editor: Michael Schwartzentruber
Interior design: Verena Velten
Cover design: Margaret Kyle
Proofreader: Dianne Greenslade

 WoodLake is an imprint of Wood Lake Publishing, Inc. Wood Lake Publishing acknowledges the financial support of the Government of Canada, through the Book Publishing Industry Development Program (BPIDP) for its publishing activities. Wood Lake Publishing also acknowledges the financial support of the Province of British Columbia through the Book Publishing Tax Credit.

At Wood Lake Publishing, we practise what we publish, being guided by a concern for fairness, justice, and equal opportunity in all of our relationships with employees and customers. Wood Lake Publishing is an employee-owned company, committed to caring for the environment and all creation. Wood Lake Publishing recycles, reuses, and encourages readers to do the same. Resources are printed on 100% post-consumer recycled paper and more environmentally friendly groundwood papers (newsprint), whenever possible. A percentage of all profit is donated to charitable organizations.

Library and Archives Canada Cataloguing in Publication
Milton, Ralph
Lectionary story Bible: year A/Ralph Milton; with the art of Margaret Kyle.
Includes index.
ISBN 978-1-55145-547-1
1. Bible stories, English. I. Kyle, Margaret II. Title.
III. Title: Story Bible.
BS551.3.M54 2007   j220.9'505   C2007-901279-5

Published by WoodLake
An imprint of Wood Lake Publishing Inc.
9590 Jim Bailey Road, Kelowna, BC, Canada, V4V 1R2
www.woodlakebooks.com
250.766.2778

Printing 10 9 8 7 6 5 4 3 2 1
Printed in China
by WKT

Contents

Introduction: Have Fun!......................7
The Church Year and the Lectionary .. 10

Making Ploughs out of Swords 13
Andrew Goes to the Temple 17
God's Beautiful Dream....................... 21
John Says, "Get Ready!"..................... 24
Isaiah's Song 27
You Are Just as Important................. 31
A Child Named Immanuel 33
Joseph's Brave Choice 35
The Light of the World....................... 37
Sing and Laugh for God 38
Run Away from King Herod 40
The Magi Visit Jesus.......................... 42
Cornelius Becomes a Christian........... 44
John Baptizes Jesus 47
Paul Writes a Letter 48
Hard as a Rock and Soft as a Sheep 51
Singing and Fishing for God.............. 52
Simon Gets a New Job 55
God Speaks through Micah 57
Jesus Teaches 58
Just Like Salt..................................... 60

The Things Jesus Taught.................... 63
Building a Good Strong House 64
Change Your Enemy into a Friend 65
God Is Like a Loving Mother.............. 67
Stop Worrying, Start Thinking........... 68
How to Build a Strong House 70
Moses Goes to Visit God 72
Jesus on the Mountaintop 74
God's Beautiful Garden 76
Jesus Gets Ready 78
Abraham and Sarah Begin a Journey.. 80
Nicodemus Comes to See Jesus 82
The Woman at the Well 84
Jesus Heals a Blind Man 87
Lazarus Is Alive! 89
Jesus Gets Ready to Die 91
Mary of Magdala Sees Jesus.............. 98
Thomas Asks Questions.................... 100
On the Road to Emmaus 102
God Is My Shepherd..........................105
Susanna Has a Good Idea.................106

A Letter to the People of the Way 108
A Room in God's House 110
The God with No Name 112
Jesus' Friends Feel Stronger 114
The Birthday of the Church...............116
How to Be a Strong Church 118
God Makes a Universe 121
A Song from the Bible.................... 123
God Makes a Promise 124
The Long Journey of
     Abraham and Sarah 128
Matthew's Surprise......................... 130
Jesus Helps a Sick Girl 131
A Mother of Nations 133
Telling the Stories of Jesus 135
Hagar Hears God's Promise...............139
Jesus Teaches His Friends 141
Abraham Doesn't Understand 142
Abigail Does Something for God........145
Rebekah and Isaac 147
Children Know This 150
Rebekah and Her Babies 152
Stories That Help Us Grow 154
Jacob Steals from Esau......................156
Jacob's Dream 159
The Wheat and the Weeds 162
Jacob Falls in Love 164
Stories of God's Shalom.....................166
Jacob Fights with God 168
Rachel Dies Having a Baby 170
A Child Helps Jesus 173
Joseph's Beautiful Coat 174
God Speaks in a Whisper..................177
Peter Walks on the Water..................178
Joseph Helps the Pharaoh 181
Joseph and His Brothers....................182
A Woman Teaches Jesus 184

Miriam Saves Her Brother.................186
Simon Becomes Peter........................189
Moses Kills a Man 191
Moses Goes Back to Egypt 194
Going to School 196
The Hebrews Leave Egypt 198
How to Fix a Problem 200
A Long, Long Journey...................... 203
Over and Over and Over and Over.... 205
I'm So Hungry!................................ 206
The Kind Farmer 207
We Want a Drink! 209
The Sister and the Brother............... 211
The Ten Commandments 213
God's Beautiful Sky 215
Keep Your Promise! 216
The People Do a Bad Thing...............218
The Best Bar Mitzvah 220
Moses Sees God............................... 222
Trouble for Jesus 224
Moses Sees a New Land................... 226
The Most Important Things 228
The People Claim the Promised Land.. 229
Jesus Turns Things Upside Down......231
The People of Israel Remember 232
Amos, the Farmer Prophet 234
The Wedding Party........................... 236
A Mother for Israel 238
An Upside Down Story..................... 240
Being Kind to God 242
Singing for God 244
The Whole Earth Says Thanks 246
Saying "Thank You" to God 248

Movements to "A Song from the Bible"
     by Keri Wehlander 250
Lectionary Index 251

Have Fun!

A word to parents and leaders

The Bible is full of stories – from heroic sagas, to knee-slapping humour, to romance and mystery. It's the *stories* in the Bible that appeal to children most and that appeal to *me* most. I think that's the part of the Bible most adults delight in, too, even though they may not admit it.

The lectionary

This is the first volume in a series of three *Lectionary Story Bibles* based on scripture readings from the *Revised Common Lectionary* (RCL). These books are designed for those who would like to supplement a lectionary-based Christian education resource, such as *Seasons of the Spirit,* or for those who would like to read stories at home to supplement their church experience.

A lectionary provides an ordered system of reading the Bible, with two readings from the Hebrew scriptures (sometimes called the Old Testament) and two readings each week from the Christian scriptures (traditionally called the New Testament).

Different denominations use different versions of the lectionary. Some of the stories included in this book may not be included in the scripture readings listed in the version of the lectionary used by your church.

You may be familiar with *The Family Story Bible.* It's a collection of stories that are presented in the order in which they appear in the Bible. All of those stories are included in this series of three *Lectionary Story Bibles.* Here they are presented in the order in which they appear in the lectionary, along with new stories based on other scripture readings from the lectionary – about three times as many as in *The Family Story Bible.*

Be like a child

A lectionary is a very useful tool, but it was designed by folks who were more concerned about the teachings of the Bible than about the stories. In other words, it was designed for adults. Sometimes it skips over the tops of stories, or picks out a few short passages from a longer, exciting saga. That's why, in many cases, my stories are based on more of the text than is recommended by the lectionary.

I try to tell the story from beginning to end, even when the scripture passages suggested by the lectionary don't. That's also why you'll find stories in this book that are in the Bible but not in the lectionary. I've tried to fill in the blanks.

The Bible is not a book of rules or a set of moral precepts that we somehow absorb and then order our lives by, although some contemporary churches encourage this view. Traditional Christianity says that when we're open to the "word of God," God will speak to us *through* the Bible. So I'm asking you to approach the Bible with a kind of childlike openness.

Jesus said it first: "Unless you become like a little child, you cannot enter God's realm" (Matthew 18:3).

Imagination and passion

I'm a storyteller, not a theologian or a Bible scholar. The two most important things I bring to the task of telling Bible stories for children are imagination and passion.

First, imagination.

Where the terse biblical text offers little detail, I add my own. Where names are missing, I invent them. Where connecting narrative is absent, I supply it. Then I add my own dash of drama and suspense and fun. Sometimes, almost the whole story comes from my imagination and almost none

of it from the Bible, though I've tried very hard to preserve the *intention* of the scripture reading.

As a professional writer, my imagination is not tamed, but it *is* disciplined. I do my research. The details I imagine are checked to make sure they have textual, historical, and theological validity. I've taken many biblical courses, done graduate work in Israel, and read hundreds of books in order to be able to do this. But still, the imagination that weaves these stories out of the raw material of the Bible is wild and childlike, and some people will find that profoundly disturbing.

Second, passion.

I believe with a deep and profound passion that God wants us to be a joyful, just, and caring people. One of the ways (but by no means the *only* way) God chose to help us be that kind of people was to encourage a particular people (the Hebrews) at a particular time (the biblical era) to record the stories of their struggles and sorrows, their joys and hopes.

They collected all kinds of writings – legends, folklore, stories, poems, fiction, history, recipes, and laws, and a dash here and there of utter drivel – into a book which we call the Bible.

The Bible can be a source of insight and wisdom and fun for adults and children. If we're open, God can speak to us through the stories of the Bible.

And when God speaks, it's never boring.

So enjoy each story, whether you think it is historically true, pure fiction, or somewhere in between. The inner truth, the wisdom, lives *inside* the story. Don't look for some pious little moral, but be open to a flash of insight into what it means to be spiritual human beings who live in families and communities with other spiritual human beings.

Let God speak to the child in you. Enjoy!

Thanks

It's always impossible to thank all those involved in a project like this. For instance, there are all the folks who have offered appreciation and helpful comments about *The Family Story Bible* and who have made it a bestseller.

Specific thanks go to Zoë, my granddaughter, who offered helpful comments about many of the stories; to my life partner, Bev, who, as always, is my first, best, and toughest critic; to Mike Schwartzentruber, editor of Wood Lake Publishing, for his editing; and to Cathie Talbot, editor of *Seasons of the Spirit*, who read all the stories and offered wise and helpful comments.

But the biggest word of thanks goes to Margaret Kyle for the inspired artwork she has provided. She has taken this book (as she did with *The Family Story Bible*) from being acceptable to being exceptional.

– R.M.

I want to thank *all* my colleagues at Wood Lake Publishing, and its co-founder Ralph Milton, for the opportunity to illustrate these stories. In my case, it is a little about being in the right place at the right time.

Ralph has a way of finding the loving and gentle heart in even the most difficult Bible stories, and then of connecting that to life in a way in which children and adults can relate. My aim was not to illustrate every aspect of the story, but to paint one or two images symbolizing this loving and gentle heart.

A special thank you to Keri Wehlander for dancing the psalm on page 123, which led to the illustrations on page 250.

I would also like to than my husband and managing editor at Wood Lake Publishing, Michael Schwartzentruber, for his honest feedback, as well as his patience. I value his wisdom and insight.

I would like to dedicate this volume to our children: Jeff, Anna, and Spiro.

– M.K.

The Seasons of the Church Year and the Lectionary

The pages in this book are colour-coded to match the seasons of the church year:

Advent – *blue*
Christmas/Epiphany – *gold/white*
The Season after Epiphany – *green*
Lent – *purple*
Easter – *gold/white*
Pentecost – *red*
The Season after Pentecost – *green*

The seasons of the church year form a unique rhythm by which Christians can live their lives. The rhythm follows the flow of the life of Jesus and is further enhanced by the melody of a lectionary which establishes a sequence of scriptures over the liturgical seasons.

The year begins with **Advent**, four Sundays leading up to Christmas Day. These four weeks invite us to prepare ourselves spiritually for the birth of Jesus. Blue, representing hope, is often used as the symbolic colour of this season.

The season of **Christmas** begins the evening of December 24, and lasts for 12 days. This is a joyous season, celebrating the birth of Jesus through to the arrival of the magi at the feast of the **Epiphany** (January 6). White and gold suggest joy and glory.

The time from the Epiphany until the beginning of Lent is the **Season after the Epiphany** or Ordinary Time. The colour green, for growth and new life, serves as a backdrop for stories of the call of disciples and prophets, and of the beginnings of Jesus' ministry.

Lent consists of the 40 days before Easter. Because each Sunday is a little Easter, these days were not included in the counting. Lent is one of the oldest observances in the church's history. In ancient times when baptisms were held annually at Easter, candidates for baptism were required to spend some time in preparation. The 40 days of Lent compared to the 40 days that Jesus spent in the wilderness prior to his ministry. Over time, this period of fasting and reflection prior to Easter became popular for all Christians. The colour purple supports a mood of penitence.

Lent ends with Palm/Passion Sunday and Holy Week – a time to remember Jesus' arrest, trial, and crucifixtion. Palm/Passion Sunday, on the 6th week of Lent is symbolized by the colour red.

After confronting the reality of crucifixion, Christians can exalt in the unbridled joy of resurrection at **Easter.** This great joyous season goes for 50 days celebrating that Christ is risen. The season reaches a wonderful conclusion with the feast of **Pentecost**, celebrating the presence of the Holy Spirit and the birth of the church. Traditionally, bright reds and oranges light up this day.

After the day of Pentecost we return to Ordinary Time – the **Season after Pentecost.** It generally covers about half the year, taking us back to Advent where the cycle begins again. In this lengthy season, we remember again the presence of God with us in the everyday.

Making Ploughs out of Swords

BASED ON ISAIAH 2:1–5

Note to leaders: This is the first in a series of four stories called "Rebekah and Her Friend Isaiah." They are based on the readings from the book of Isaiah during the Season of Advent.

Isaiah was a prophet who lived a very long time ago.

A prophet is like someone who takes your temperature. That person can tell if you are well or if you are sick and need some medicine.

A prophet looks at things that are happening in our city or in our country, and then tells us if our city or our country is well or if it is sick and needs some things to be changed. A prophet helps us know if we are living the way God wants us to live.

Isaiah was a prophet like that. Everybody called him Old Isaiah. They said it as if it was just one word: "Oldisaiah." "Hi, Oldisaiah," they'd say, when they saw him in the afternoons sitting under his favourite tree.

Old Isaiah had many friends, but his best friends were children. His very special best friend was Rebekah. Sometimes Rebekah would give Old Isaiah a kiss on the forehead. "He is so hairy everywhere else," she said. And then Old Isaiah would take her hand and hold it up to his hairy cheek and press it gently.

That's what Old Isaiah did when Rebekah told him she was going to be a big sister. "My mom is going to have a baby!" she said.

"Every baby needs a big sister like you," he said. Then Old Isaiah smiled the biggest smile Rebekah had ever seen. His smile showed all his teeth, except where he didn't have any.

Each morning Old Isaiah went to the marketplace. He would sit on a big rock in the middle of the market. And he would talk to anyone who would listen.

There were always lots of people in the marketplace. Some of them paid no attention to Old Isaiah. Some of them would listen. Some would yell angry words at him.

"Why do you say things that make people angry?" Rebekah asked him once.

"Because I can't help it," he said. "When I feel God is giving me things to say, I have to say them. I have to tell people what God wants them to hear."

One morning when Isaiah was talking in the marketplace, two men started yelling at each other.

Old Isaiah stopped talking. Rebekah was standing nearby. "What are the men so angry about?" she asked him. Old Isaiah didn't hear her. Or at least, he didn't answer. He was looking at the two men and Rebekah could see fire in his eyes.

Then the two men took big swords and started fighting. They really hurt each other. One man had a big bleeding cut on his hip. The other man had a big bleeding cut on his shoulder. They both fell down. They were so hurt they couldn't fight anymore. Finally, some women came to help them.

Old Isaiah saw the two swords lying on the ground. He walked over to where the two men had been fighting. "Give me those swords!" he roared. Rebekah had never seen him like this. She could see that when Old Isaiah was angry he could yell loudly and walk fast. "Give me those swords!" he roared again. "God hates all the things we use to hurt each other."

Then Old Isaiah held the swords up high as he walked through the crowd. He walked right up to Amoz, the blacksmith.

"Here," Old Isaiah said. "Take these swords and make them into ploughs."

"But I can't," said Amoz. "They belong to the men who were fighting."

"Do it!" roared Old Isaiah.

Amoz took a sword and pushed it into a very hot fire. When the sword glowed bright red, he laid it on a big iron block called an anvil. He pounded the sword with a big hammer. He pounded and pounded. Soon it wasn't a sword anymore. It was a plough that could be used to dig in the ground and grow things.

Old Isaiah took the two ploughs and started banging them together so they made a loud ringing noise. Soon everyone was quiet, and Old Isaiah started to speak.

"My friends," he said softly. "God doesn't want you to have things like swords. Take your swords to the blacksmith and make them into ploughs like these. Then you can use them to grow food.

"Listen to what God is telling you," he said. Old Isaiah spoke very softly and gently. Everyone was so quiet they could hear each word. "God doesn't want you to fight. God wants you to love each other and to work together."

Old Isaiah left the market and walked slowly to his place under the big old tree. Only Rebekah went with him. "I'm very tired," he said to her. "I think I need to have a little sleep."

"When you wake up," asked Rebekah, "will you write about this in your book?'

"Oh, yes," said Old Isaiah. "And this is what I will write." He closed his eyes and the words he spoke sounded to Rebekah a little bit like a song.

> A great leader will come to you,
> a leader who will teach us new ways –
> a leader who will teach us how to be kind.
> And then everyone,
> yes, everyone,
> will beat their swords into ploughs.
> They will make garden tools from their spears.
> They will not fight with each other anymore
> and they won't teach each other how to fight.
> A great leader will come to you.
> Get ready. Get ready.

Andrew Goes to the Temple

BASED ON PSALM 122

Andrew was 11. "Almost 12," he liked to say. And he was really excited.

Andrew was going with his mom and dad to Jerusalem. He had been to Jerusalem lots of times before because it was only a short walk from where he lived in Bethany. But this time, Andrew's parents were going to take him to the temple. He had never been inside the temple before.

The temple was like a very big, very special church. Andrew was really excited about going there, because everyone said it was so beautiful. Andrew's mom and dad went to the temple in Jerusalem at least once a year. "We want to show you the temple so you can get used to it a little. When we go back again, we'll have a special celebration there for you, Andrew. Then you will no longer be a child. You will be an adult."

Andrew went with his family every Sabbath to his own church in Bethany. It was called a synagogue. In the synagogue, they heard stories and they learned songs about God. Andrew liked going to the synagogue because all the people of Bethany went there every week. The best part was the lunch they served after every synagogue service.

But this was different. This was exciting!

"We sing a special song when we walk," said Andrew's mom. "It only takes half an hour to walk to Jerusalem, but it's fun to sing when we walk, and it gets us ready to pray to God when we get to the temple."

And so Andrew's mom, whose name was Martha, and his dad, whose name was Simon, began to sing.

> I was glad when they said,
> "let us go to the house,
> let us go to the house of our God."

"I'll sing it again, Andrew," said Simon. "Sing along with me as much as you can."

"It's easier to sing along with mom," said Andrew. "Her voice is high like mine."

"Whatever works," smiled his dad. "You can sing the chorus along with your mom, and I'll sing some of the verses in between. Here's the first verse."

> I was so glad when they told me to come,
> And now I'm standing here.
> I'm standing here in the house of our God,
> I'm filled with hope and cheer.

Right away Martha sang the chorus, and Andrew sang along as much as he could remember.

> I was glad when they said,
> "let us go to the house,
> let us go to the house of our God."

Then Simon, in his strong, warm voice, sang another verse.

> And so we come to the house of our God,
> We come to pray and to sing,
> We walk along to the house of our God,
> Holding the gifts that we bring.

"What gifts?" Andrew asked. "We take money to our synagogue every Sabbath. Do we have to bring money to the temple too?"

"We don't have to," said his father. "We want to. Because God loves us and is so good to us, we like to bring gifts that help God's people."

Martha gave Andrew a little hug. "You have so many questions, Andrew. That's good." Then she began to sing the chorus of their song again.

> I was glad when they said,
> "let us go to the house,
> let us go to the house of our God."

This time Andrew sang the whole chorus right through with his mom. And he hummed along while his dad sang the next verse.

> We always pray for the house of our God,
> May those who gather find peace.
> We pray and sing in the house of our God,
> May our love and joy increase.

And then they sang the chorus again. This time, all three sang it together, and Andrew was surprised when his voice suddenly changed in a funny kind of way and he sang part of the chorus in low notes like his dad. Then it was up high again like his mom's.

This time his dad gave Andrew a little hug. "Your voice is changing, my son. Soon, much too soon, you will no longer be a child."

Then Andrew and his family came to the top of a small hill. They could see Jerusalem and the temple, shinning like a jewel in the middle of the city.

Andrew was very excited.

God's Beautiful Dream

BASED ON ISAIAH 11:1–10

Note to leaders: This is the second in a series of four stories called "Rebekah and Her Friend Isaiah." If you are reading this to children who have not heard the first story, you may wish to introduce this story by reading the first four paragraphs of "Making Ploughs out of Swords" (see page 13).

Old Isaiah had a long grey beard. Sometimes, when he got angry or excited, he could lift his head high and walk fast. In the market, when many people were listening, Old Isaiah could talk very loudly.

But then he would be very tired. He walked slowly and needed a heavy stick to keep him from falling.

Some of the children in Jerusalem would yell bad things at him as he walked by. Old Isaiah pretended he couldn't hear them.

But most of the children knew that he was a kind old man who liked to talk with them. Even though he could never remember their names.

Sometimes Old Isaiah didn't want anyone around. Sometimes he would just sit under his big tree, with his eyes closed. Some people said he was sleeping, but the children knew that he was dreaming. Or thinking. Or praying.

"Sometimes the dream I have is God's dream," he told Rebekah one day.

Rebekah had just lost one of her front baby teeth. Isaiah looked at the place where the tooth had been. He looked very carefully. Isaiah knew such things were important.

"How do you know when it is God's dream?" Rebekah asked. She sat down on the grass beside Isaiah. She leaned against him a little. Old Isaiah always smelled a bit like the medicine he took for his sore bones.

"When I have a dream like the one I just had, it fills me up inside so my whole body tingles. It feels as if God loves every bit of me, from my toes right up to my grey hair. I feel so warm and so strong inside, I just know that the dream I am having is God's dream."

"Were there children in your dream? Or animals?"

"No. Maybe there should be. The dream God gave me is about a leader. This person would really want to lead in God's way. Such a leader would really care about poor people. Things should be changed so no one has to be poor anymore."

"Do you think this leader would care about children? And about animals? Some leaders don't care about them very much."

"That's true, Rebekah. It's very sad, but true. And I think maybe God's dream isn't finished yet. Could you help me dream some more of it?"

"Sure!" said Rebekah. She closed her eyes and leaned against Old Isaiah and tried to feel a little bit lazy – as if she were going to sleep. Old Isaiah closed his eyes, too. They sat together and dreamed for a long time.

Then Rebekah spoke very quietly. "I had a little bit of a dream about a wolf with big sharp teeth. And a tiny newborn lamb. They were playing together. They were friends."

After a while, Old Isaiah spoke. "I dreamed of a cow and a bear together. And the bear was eating grass just like the cow, so the cow wasn't afraid. And then I saw a lion eating straw."

"I was dreaming about a tiny baby," said Rebekah. "Like the baby my mom is going to have. The baby was just learning to crawl. It was playing right near some snakes. The baby picked them up, but the snakes didn't bite."

"Yes! That's it! A child!" Isaiah's eyes flew open. "A child just your age, Rebekah."

"Was I in your dream?" she asked.

"Well, not you, Rebekah. But it was a child like you. In my part of God's dream, I saw a child your age helping people understand how to live in peace. I want to write that in my book, Rebekah.

"I will write God's dream about peace – about how people who always fight with each other can be kind to each other. They can learn to love each other. To play together. To work together.

"And just the way you helped me now, I will write about how a small child will teach people how to be kind to each other."

Rebekah stood up and gave Old Isaiah a kiss. He took her hand and held it next to his wrinkled cheek. "You're a wonderful person, Rebekah," he said.

Then Old Isaiah smiled his big, toothy smile. And Rebekah laughed. "Old Isaiah! You have holes in your mouth where teeth should be. Just like me!"

Here's what Old Isaiah wrote in his book.

A child shall be born for my people,
a child full of wisdom and hope.
This child will grow up full of wisdom,
bringing justice and peace to the world.
And the wolf and the lamb will play,
the cow and the bear will eat grass,
the lion will eat straw like the ox,
and a baby will play with snakes.
People will no longer hurt each other,
and the earth will be covered with love.

John Says, "Get Ready!"

BASED ON MATTHEW 3:1–12

Do you remember John? John was just a little bit older than Jesus. John's mother, Elizabeth, and Jesus' mother, Mary, were cousins. Mary went to visit Elizabeth just before John was born.

Some people thought John was weird. He wore clothes made from the hair of camels. He ate insects and wild honey.

Not only that, John often sounded angry. Sometimes he even yelled at people.

But John had an important job to do. God wanted John to get people ready for the Messiah, the one who would tell people about God's love.

"Get ready," John shouted. "If you have done wrong things, tell God you are sorry! Live in God's way!"

"What do you mean?" people asked John.

"If you have two coats, share with someone who doesn't have any. Be honest. Be kind to others. Don't be greedy."

Many people came to John. "We are sorry for the bad things we've done," they said. "We want to live God's way."

So John baptized them in the river. John held them under the water for just a moment. Then he lifted them up again.

"I feel washed clean," they said. "I feel clean inside."

"I baptize you with water," John told the people. "But someone is coming who will baptize with something much better. You will be baptized by God's spirit.

"It won't be with water. You will feel God's spirit. It will feel like a nice warm fire inside you.

"When this special someone comes, you will know that you are one of God's children."

Isaiah's Song

BASED ON ISAIAH 35:1–10

Note to leaders: This is the third in a series of four stories called "Rebekah and Her Friend Isaiah." If you are reading this to children who have not heard the first two stories, you may wish to introduce this story by reading the first four paragraphs of "Making Ploughs out of Swords" (see page 13).

Rebekah and Nathaniel were on their way home from a friend's house. They waved to Old Isaiah, who was sitting under his tree.

Old Isaiah jumped right up. Well, he jumped up as fast as he could. He started waving to Nathaniel and Rebekah. "Come children. Quickly! Quickly!"

"What's the matter?" asked Rebekah.

"I need your help!" said Old Isaiah. His face was a little bit red and he was breathing hard.

"Are you sick?" asked Nathaniel.

"Sick? Oh no. No. I'm as well as any old man can be. But I need your help with something really important. I had another dream!"

"Was it God's dream again, with animals and children?" asked Rebekah.

"Well, no. But yes! Let me sit down so my poor old brain can think." Old Isaiah sat back down on the grass. Rebekah could tell he was excited because he moved quickly. Usually, Old Isaiah would sit down slowly and talk about his "sore bones."

"It was God's dream, yes. But not about animals and children this time. It was a song. A beautiful song!"

"Can you sing it for us?" Nathaniel asked.

"That's the problem," said Isaiah. "When I was a young man, I could really sing. Now I sound like a sick horse."

"I don't sing either," said Nathaniel sadly. "My dad says I always hit the wrong notes."

"I know how to sing," said Rebekah.

"I need you both to help," said Old Isaiah. "Here are the words for the first part of the song.

> The desert will sing and the flowers will bloom,
> All God's creatures will sing and be glad.

"How do I know what notes to sing?" asked Rebekah.

"That's the problem. I don't have any notes," said Old Isaiah. "Nathaniel, I've seen you dance sometimes. I've seen you move your body while other people sing. So I'll keep saying the words over and over, and you move your body. Move it any way that it feels right.

"And Rebekah. Listen to the words and watch Nathaniel, and then sing any music that feels right."

Over and over, about ten times, Old Isaiah said the words and Nathaniel danced and Rebekah sang notes. After a while, it started to sound like a real song.

"Here's some more words," said Old Isaiah.

> Those who are weak will soon become strong,
> Those who cry will no longer be sad.

This time it was easier. Old Isaiah said the words out loud over and over. Nathaniel danced. He tried to make his arms and legs and body be weak and then strong, crying, then happy. They only had to do it five times before Rebekah had a good song.

"This is fun!" said Nathaniel.

"It's wonderful!" said Old Isaiah. "Now here's the last part...

> Then the eyes of the blind will be opened again
> And those who are deaf will hear songs.

This time, they only had to do it three times. Old Isaiah spoke. Nathaniel danced. Rebekah sang.

Then all of them sang the whole song all over again, three times. "You can sing, Nathaniel," said Rebekah. "You sang all the right notes!"

Old Isaiah was smiling his big toothy smile. "This is the way it should be," he said. "When God's people help each other, wonderful things happen.

"That's what I am going to write in my book. When God's messenger comes, that's the way we will do things. We will all work together with God. We will make a beautiful world."

ADVENT 3

You Are Just as Important

BASED ON MATTHEW 11:2–11

*Note to leaders: One of the readings suggested for this Sunday is Luke 1:47–55.
It is the "Magnificat," the song that Mary sings when she visits her cousin Elizabeth.
It is paraphrased for children in The Family Story Bible, page 159.*

The prophet named John travelled to many places in Israel. He helped people understand how to live God's way.

"I have a message from God!" John said. "A very important person is coming. Someone who will show you what God is like."

Many, many people gathered to hear John talk about this wonderful person. When the King of Israel heard about it, he was afraid. "If this kind of person is coming, he might want to be king instead of me. Tell John to stop talking about it!"

But John didn't stop. He couldn't stop. "I have to say what God tells me to say!" So the king locked John into jail.

After John had been in jail for a long time, somebody told him that Jesus was going to different places in Israel. Jesus was telling people how much God loved them. He was showing them how to live God's way.

So John sent a message to Jesus. "Are you the one we have been waiting for? Are you the person God told me about?"

Jesus smiled when he heard John's message. "Go tell John what you see happening. Tell him blind people can see, deaf people can hear. Tell John that people with sore legs and feet can walk again. Poor people hear the good news that God loves them very much, too."

Then Jesus talked to the people gathered around him. "Do you remember John? He was sometimes called 'the baptizer,' because he often baptized people in the river. That's where he baptized me. There is nobody in the whole world that is more important than John! Nobody!"

Then Jesus took the hand of a child. "But here is a wonderful surprise." He lifted the child up into his arms. "God loves you very much," Jesus said to the child. "God thinks you are just as important as the prophet John."

A Child Named Immanuel

BASED ON ISAIAH 7:10–16

Note to leaders: This is the final story in a series of four stories called "Rebekah and Her Friend Isaiah." If you are reading this to children who have not heard any of the previous stories, you may wish to introduce this story by reading the first six paragraphs of "Making Ploughs out of Swords" (see page 13).

Rebekah was so excited.

The new baby sister she had been waiting for had finally come. Rebekah got to hold the new child very soon after it was born.

Rebekah invited Nathaniel and all her other friends to come and see. They all said it was a very beautiful baby. Rebekah just smiled. She already knew that.

Then Rebekah asked her mom, "Can I take our new baby to visit Old Isaiah? Please!"

"You can, if I can come with you," said her mom. "Just to be sure everything is all right."

So the next morning, when it was still cool outside, Rebekah wrapped the new baby in a blanket. She and her mom carried the child to the big old tree. Old Isaiah was sitting there, writing his book, just as Rebekah knew he would be.

"Look, Old Isaiah," she said. "Look at this beautiful new baby. I'm the baby's big sister."

"That's good. Every new baby needs a big sister like you, Rebekah." Old Isaiah's eyes looked kind of watery. Rebekah wondered if he was going to cry. "Could I hold the baby just for a little bit?" he asked.

Rebekah looked at her mother, who nodded, "Yes." So Old Isaiah took the tiny child in his arms. He looked into the eyes of the baby for a long time. Then Rebekah and her mother saw a wonderful, happy smile come to Old Isaiah's face. And they could see happy tears in his eyes as the new baby smiled up at him.

Then, in a whisper, he said to Rebekah, "This is how it must be. Don't you see? Now I know how God's new leader will come to us. A young woman, like your mother, will have a child. And she will call the child 'Immanuel.' God's message will not be some words in a book. A tiny baby will be God's message to us!"

"Immanuel?" Rebekah asked.

"Yes, Immanuel. It means, 'God is with us.' That will be God's sign. That will be God's way of saying, 'I love you!' And as this baby grows, people will know more and more about what God is like. That's why the baby will be called Immanuel."

"Mom," said Rebekah. "Could we name our new baby Immanuel?"

"That's a really nice idea," said Rebekah's mom. "Except that our baby already has a name. But sometimes when you are singing the baby to sleep, you can use the name Immanuel. Would that be okay, Old Isaiah?"

"Oh yes," he said, smiling his big, toothy grin. But there were still tears in his eyes. "I think every new baby should be called Immanuel sometimes. Because we can see a little bit of God in every child. Sometimes I think God wants us grownups to become a little like children, so we can really feel God's love. Thank you so much for bringing your baby for a visit, Rebekah. Now I know what to write in my book about God's dream for us."

As Rebekah and the baby and their mom walked back home, Old Isaiah went back to his book.

And he wrote:

> Look! Listen!
> A young woman
> is going to have a new baby.
> And she will call the child "Immanuel,"
> which means, "God is with us!"
> And that baby will be God's greatest gift –
> God's message of love to us all.

ADVENT 4

Joseph's Brave Choice

BASED ON MATTHEW 1:18–25 AND LUKE 1:26–38

Note to leaders: If you are talking about the birth of Jesus on this Sunday, you may wish to use the story for Christmas Day. Additional birth stories may be found in The Family Story Bible, *pages 156, 161, and 163.*

This is how the birth of Jesus took place.

Mary and Joseph lived in a small town called Nazareth. They were planning to marry each other.

But before their wedding day arrived, Mary learned that God had chosen her to have a very special baby.

When Joseph heard about this, he was very worried. "How can Mary have a baby when we aren't married yet?" he wondered. "What will people think of me? What will people think of Mary?" In those days, people got angry when women had babies before they were married. Joseph was afraid people would hurt Mary because she was pregnant.

Then one night, Joseph had a dream. He dreamed that an angel was telling him, "Don't worry, Joseph. It's all right. You and Mary go ahead and get married just as you planned."

So Mary and Joseph got married, and they loved each other very much.

Joseph made a cradle so that he could rock the baby to sleep. "Look Mary," he said. "I can make the cradle rock just with my foot. Then I can carve things out of wood with my hands, I can sing to the baby, and I can rock the baby with my foot."

Mary smiled and touched Joseph's hand. "You love the baby, even though it isn't born yet, don't you?" She took Joseph's hand and put it gently on her tummy where the baby was growing inside. "Can you feel the baby move?" she asked.

"Oh yes, yes! I can!" Joseph looked very surprised and he had happy tears in his eyes. "Will it be a girl or a boy, Mary?"

"It will be what God sends us."

"Yes. Whether the baby is a girl or a boy, whether it is big or little, whether it is strong or very weak, it will be God's gift. And we already love the baby. So we will be happy when it is born."

Together Joseph and Mary planned and worked to make a loving home for their special baby. And when the baby was finally born, Mary and Joseph named him Jesus.

The Light of the World

BASED ON JOHN 1:1–14

Note to leaders: *If you are looking for more traditional stories about the birth of Jesus, you can find them in* The Family Story Bible, *pages 161 and 163.*

Imagine a long, long time ago when there was no world. No stars. No animals. No people. No you.

Just nothing.

Now imagine that even though there was nothing, God was there.

God was there like a strange light that is everywhere, but doesn't come from anywhere. The light didn't shine on anything, because there was nothing to shine on. Can you imagine that?

Then God had an idea. God decided to make the universe, and the earth, and to fill it with all kinds of creatures, and with all kinds of people like you and me. And in each person, and in every living thing, and in everything God created, God put some of the light that was there before there was anything. You have some of that light in you. People can see that light shining in your eyes when you laugh. Sometimes they also see God's light when you cry.

Then God had a very special idea about a very special person. God decided to make a person who would come and live with us to show us what God is like. A special person to show us how to live God's way.

There was a man named John. God sent John to tell us about the very special person that was coming.

"Look," said John. "You can't see God because God isn't a 'something' you can see. Nobody can see God. But God will send us a person to show us what God is like. God will send this special person to tell us about that wonderful light that all of us have – God's light that comes to us from the time before there was anything.

"The name of that special person is Jesus. Jesus will help you shine. Jesus will help you find God's light that is inside you. Jesus will help you live God's way."

Sing and Laugh for God

BASED ON PSALM 148

In the Bible, we find many songs that people long ago liked to sing. Some of the songs were about sad things that happened. But this one, which is called Psalm 148, is a very happy song.

We have the words to the song, but we don't have the music. So as you say these words, you could make up your own music to go with them.

Look up at the sky and sing,
Look up at all the birds!
God has given you your life.
Sing and laugh for God.

Can you see the sun and moon?
Can you see the sky?
The song they sing is meant for God.
Why don't you sing it, too?

The whales and fishes laugh for God!
Snow and rain laugh, too!
All the hills and mountains laugh!
Why don't you laugh, too?

Queens and kings will smile for God!
Old men and women grin.
Children and their parents smile.
Why don't you smile, too?

If you breathe then you can sing.
Sing your song to God.
God has given you your life.
Sing and laugh for God.

Run Away from King Herod

BASED ON MATTHEW 2:13–23

Note to leaders: In the Revised Common Lectionary, *which this book follows, the flight to Egypt is listed for the first Sunday after Christmas, and the visit of the Magi (Matthew 2:1–12) for the Sunday following. This order reverses the natural flow of the story. Please make whatever adaptations or explanations you feel are necessary.*

After Jesus was born, Mary and Joseph stayed in Bethlehem. They were waiting for Jesus to get stronger before they went back to their home in Nazareth.

One night, after Mary and Joseph had kissed Jesus "Good night," they went to sleep. But Joseph couldn't sleep very well.

"I had a scary dream," Joseph said to Mary in the morning. "In my dream, I heard God tell me to take you and Jesus and run away to Egypt. King Herod thinks Jesus will grow up to become king instead of him. Now Herod wants to kill Jesus!"

"That's terrible!" said Mary. "But do we have to go to Egypt? It is so far away and we don't have any friends or family there. It will be awful!"

"I know," said Joseph. "But we have to go! And God will go with us."

So they wrapped their blankets and clothes and some food into a bundle. They put it on the back of their little donkey. Then they started walking. Mary and Joseph took turns carrying Jesus. It took many, many days to walk all that way. They were very tired and their feet hurt. Sometimes they were thirsty and hungry. But they were safe.

The day after Mary, Joseph, and Jesus left for Egypt, King Herod sent his soldiers to Bethlehem. They were looking for Jesus. They didn't know which baby was Jesus, so they just killed all the babies. It was terrible! It was such a sad time for all the families in Bethlehem.

Mary, Joseph, and Jesus stayed in Egypt a long time. Then, one morning, when Joseph woke up, he was smiling. "God spoke to me in a dream again," he told Mary. "King Herod is dead, so it's safe to go back to our home in Nazareth."

"I'll be so happy to get home," said Mary. Jesus was big enough to walk and run and play by himself. When he saw his mother smile, he smiled too.

Mary picked him up. "You're such a big boy now, Jesus. Maybe now you can walk part of the way. Or you can ride on the donkey!"

"It will be a long walk," said Joseph. "But God will go with us."

The Magi Visit Jesus

BASED ON MATTHEW 2:1–12

Note to leaders: Please see the comments about the order of these stories on page 40.

After Jesus was born, Mary and Joseph stayed in Bethlehem for a quite a while. They were waiting for Mary to feel stronger and for Jesus to get a little bigger before they went back to their home in Nazareth. Being born is very hard work for both the mother and the baby.

In a country far away, a bright star shone in the sky. Some Magi saw the star. Magi are sometimes called "wise men," or "wise ones," or "kings."

"That bright star means something important is happening," said one of the Magi. "It's happening in a faraway land. We should go and see."

"Yes," said one of the other Magi. "When a bright star appears in the sky, it means that a king is born."

So they loaded food and clothes onto their camels' backs. Then they started off. As they walked along, the star seemed to move ahead of them. "I think the star is leading us somewhere," said one of the Magi.

So they followed the star. It led them to Jerusalem. In Jerusalem, they went to see King Herod. "We have been following a bright star. We think the star is leading us to a new king who has just been born. Do you know where that king is? We brought him some gifts."

Herod began to feel afraid. Would this baby become king instead of him? Herod was very smart and didn't tell anyone he was afraid. Instead, he just smiled and said to the Magi, "I'll find out for you."

Then he left the Magi and called together all the smart people he knew. He asked them, "Do you know where this new king was born?"

"Sure we know. We have some old books that tell us these things. If a new king was born, it would have been in the town of Bethlehem."

Herod went back to the Magi. He smiled nicely to hide his fear.

"The new king was born in Bethlehem," he told them. "Isn't that wonderful? Why don't you go and find him? Give him your gifts and then come back and tell me where he is. I want to take him some gifts, too."

"We'll do that," said the Magi. "Thanks for your help."

So they went to Bethlehem, which isn't very far from Jerusalem. They gave Jesus the special gifts they had brought with them – shining gold, sweet-smelling incense, and a perfume called myrrh.

That night, one of the Magi had a dream. A really bad dream. He shook the other Magi and said, "Wake up! I had a dream that King Herod wants to hurt the baby Jesus. We must not go back to tell Herod where the baby is. We have to go back home, but we should take a different road that doesn't go by Herod's castle. We've got to leave right now!"

Cornelius Becomes a Christian

BASED ON ACTS 10:1 – 11:18

One day while Peter was praying, he saw something strange in his mind.

Peter saw a big cloth coming down from the sky. In the cloth were all kinds of animals. Some of the animals were the kind that Jewish people wouldn't eat.

Then Peter heard a voice. "Take these animals, Peter. Cook them and eat them."

"Oh no," said Peter. "I'm Jewish. Jewish people say some of those animals are unclean. We don't eat them."

"Don't say they are unclean," said the voice. "God made them."

Then the big cloth went back up to the sky. But it came back again. And again. It happened three times.

Just then, there was a knock at the door.

"I have a message for Peter," said the man at the door. "Would you come and visit Cornelius? Cornelius would like you to come and see him."

Peter stopped to think. Cornelius was a soldier. Cornelius was not Jewish. "I'm Jewish," thought Peter. "I shouldn't go into the house of someone who isn't Jewish."

Then Peter remembered the big cloth. "God made Cornelius, just like God made me," thought Peter. "I'm not unclean and neither is Cornelius. I think God wants me to go."

Cornelius was very happy when Peter got there. "Thank you for coming," he said. "Please tell me about Jesus."

So Peter told Cornelius and his whole family all about Jesus. Peter talked about the many ways Jesus had showed us how to live in God's way. "God wants us to be kind. We should never hurt each other. The power we have is the power of love."

Peter looked at Cornelius. He looked at the other people in Cornelius' family. Peter could see that the spirit of Jesus had come into their hearts.

"Would you like to be baptized?" Peter asked.

"Yes," they all said. "We want to be baptized. We want to try to live in God's way."

Some of the other Christians were angry when they heard what Peter had done. "Cornelius and his family aren't Jewish," they said. "And Cornelius is a soldier. How can they be *people of the way?*"

Peter told them about the big cloth and everything else that had happened. Then everyone understood that God's love is for everybody. They knew that Jesus came to show God's love for the whole world.

"Everyone can learn how to live in God's way," said Peter. "Everyone can be part of the Christian church."

John Baptizes Jesus

BASED ON MATTHEW 3:11–17

There was a man named John, who baptized people in the Jordan River.

People would come to hear what John had to say. "Be sorry for the wrong things you have done," he told them, "because God is getting ready to do something very special."

Some of the people would say to John, "We really do want to live God's way." Then John would baptize them. He would hold them under the water for just a little while, and say a short prayer. Then he would lift them out of the water. "You have been washed clean," he would say to them. "Now try to live the way God wants you to live."

Sometimes John would get a kind of dreamy look in his eye. "My friends," he would say, "I've baptized you with water. But I think God is going to send us someone who will baptize us in a new way. It won't be with water. It will be with God's Spirit."

One day Jesus came to hear what John was saying. "Will you please baptize me?" asked Jesus.

John's eyes got very big. Suddenly he knew that Jesus was the special person. This was the person who would baptize people in a new way.

"No, no!" John said to Jesus. "You should baptize *me* instead."

"John," said Jesus, "God wants *you* to baptize *me.*"

John took a deep breath. "Well, if you say so," he said.

So John held Jesus, and dipped him under the water for just a little while. He said a short prayer, then lifted Jesus up again.

Jesus and John and all the people who were gathered around felt God's love in a very special way. Some of them said they heard God's voice saying, "This is my child. I love him. I am really pleased with him."

Jesus knew God wanted him to tell people about God. He knew he had to show people how to live God's way.

But Jesus also knew it would be very hard to do that. So Jesus went away to a lonely place to get himself ready.

Paul Writes a Letter

BASED ON 1 CORINTHIANS 1:1–9

In the Bible, you can find some letters written by a man named Paul.

Paul didn't know Jesus when Jesus was still alive. But Paul had heard the stories about Jesus. He knew that God wanted him to tell those stories to other people.

So Paul went to a place called Corinth. He lived there for a little while, and told many people the stories about Jesus. Some of the people who heard these stories got together and started a little church.

Paul had to go to other places to tell the stories of Jesus. But he wanted to keep telling the people of Corinth how to be a church and how to live God's way.

In those days, they didn't have telephones or e-mail or airplanes. So Paul often wrote letters to the little church in Corinth. This is what he wrote in one of his letters.

This is a letter from Paul. It is a letter to the people in the church at Corinth.

You are part of many churches in many places, because you know the stories of Jesus and you are trying to live God's way.

When I think about you, I say "thank you" to God. That's because you have learned to tell other people about Jesus. You tell people how God loves them.

I know this is hard sometimes. Some people don't want to hear about Jesus. They get angry and tell you to go away. But God will help you feel strong so you can keep on telling the stories about Jesus to everyone you meet.

I am proud of you. I am so glad that you are able to keep on being a church together. Try to be kind to each other. Don't argue.

God wants you to get along with each other. That way you can help each other live in God's way.

Paul

Hard as a Rock and Soft as a Sheep

BASED ON JOHN 1:35–42

The day after Jesus was baptized he went back to the Jordan River. The prophet John was still there talking to people and baptizing those who wanted to live God's way.

When John saw Jesus coming, he shouted to all the people. "Look! Here comes the Lamb of God!"

"What do you mean, 'Lamb of God'?" asked Andrew. Andrew was one of John's special friends.

"You know about sheep and shepherds don't you, Andrew?" asked John.

Andrew nodded, "Yes."

"Well, think of God as a shepherd. The shepherd has a special love for a tiny lamb that has just been born. God loves Jesus in that special way. That's why I called Jesus, 'the Lamb of God.'"

"Then we really need to listen to Jesus," said Andrew. So he and the rest of John's friends spent the whole afternoon with Jesus. They asked questions. They listened to stories about how other people came to love God. They sang songs about how much God loves them.

"Jesus," said Andrew, "would you come and meet my brother Simon? My brother really likes stories and songs about God."

So Andrew took Jesus to meet Simon. They talked for a while. Jesus could tell that Simon wanted very badly to live God's way.

"Simon," said Jesus, "I want to give you a new name. You are a very strong person. I don't mean that you have big muscles. I mean that you are strong on the inside. You will live God's way, even when that is very hard to do. So I am going to call you Peter. Do you know what the name Peter means?"

"No," said Simon.

"Peter means 'rock.' On the inside, in your heart, you are as strong as a rock."

Andrew laughed. "Peter, you are hard and tough like a rock, and Jesus, you are soft and tender like a lamb. You two will make a good team!"

Singing and Fishing for God

BASED ON ISAIAH 9:1–4 AND MATTHEW 4:18–20

There are many songs in the Bible. We still have words for those songs, but we don't have the music. Why not say the words out loud? Then you can make up your own music to go with them.

Here are the words to one of the songs that the prophet Isaiah sang.

> The people that lived in the dark,
> those people have seen a great light.
> The people that walked in the dark,
> their life is now shiny and bright.
>
> Dear God, you have made us so glad,
> we just want to jump up and sing.
> Dear God, we can never be sad,
> your light sparkles bright in each thing.
>
> We were hurting and sad till you came,
> but now we feel strong and alive.
> We were hurting and tired till you came,
> but now we feel glad we're alive.

Many years after the prophet Isaiah sang that song, Jesus' friends found it in their Bible. They sang the song over and over, until everybody could join in.

One day, Jesus was walking beside a lake called Galilee. He saw Peter and his brother, Andrew, trying to catch fish. "Hi!" said Jesus. "Are you catching lots of fish?"

"No, not very many," said Peter.

"I have an idea," said Jesus. "Why don't you come with me and we will fish for people?"

"I don't get it!" said Andrew.

"Neither do I," said Peter.

Jesus laughed. "I'm going to go to different towns and villages and tell people how to live in God's way. I want to catch them and tell them how much God loves them. Can you help me do that?"

"Now I understand," said Andrew.

"I think that would be wonderful," said Peter.

Simon Gets a New Job

BASED ON MATTHEW 4:18–22

Simon was tired. He had been trying to catch fish all night long. But there didn't seem to be any fish.

Simon was cleaning his fishing net on the shore. He saw Jesus walking toward him. A crowd of people was following Jesus.

"Simon," called Jesus, "may I use your boat?"

"Sure," said Simon. "Why?"

"If you stop it near the shore, I can sit in your boat and talk to the people."

Jesus sat in Simon's boat. Jesus told the people about God's promise to love everyone. Simon listened, too.

When Jesus was finished talking to the people, he asked Simon, "How many fish did you catch?"

"There aren't any fish out there," Simon grumbled.

"Sure there are," laughed Jesus. "Get back into your boat and go where the water is deep. Then try again."

"Wow!" shouted Simon after he started fishing again. "Look at all these fish. My boat is full. Look out! It might sink."

It was hard to row that boat full of fish back to the shore. As he rowed, Simon thought about Jesus. He thought about the things he had just heard Jesus saying.

Then Simon felt sad. "I can't live in God's way," he thought. "I tell lies. I get angry. I'm ugly. I do stupid things. Jesus wouldn't want to be my friend."

Jesus was standing on the shore waiting for Simon. "Simon," said Jesus, "I'd like to talk to you."

"You shouldn't be talking to me," Simon said to Jesus. "I'm not a good person. I do bad things. And I'm not very smart."

"Simon," said Jesus, "I helped you with your work. Why don't you come and help me with mine?"

"But all I can do is catch fish!"

"Fine," laughed Jesus. "Come, help me catch people."

That's how Simon became one of Jesus' special helpers. Other women and men also became Jesus' special helpers.

The Bible calls them disciples.

God Speaks through Micah

BASED ON MICAH 6:1–8

Many years ago, before the time of Jesus, there was a prophet named Micah.

A prophet is someone who helps us understand how to live God's way.

The people in the place where Micah lived knew about God. They liked to sing many loud songs to God. They often had big parties, where they cooked lots of food and invited everyone to come. "We are doing this for God!" they would say.

Sometimes they made big buildings where people could come to pray to God. The buildings cost a lot of money. "See how much money I am giving!" people would say. "I am doing this for God!"

The prophet Micah didn't like this. So he asked God, "What shall I tell the people?" Micah sat very quietly, listening for what God would say.

Then Micah said to the people, "Here is what God is saying to you:

'O my people, what have I done to you?
Don't you remember all the things I did for you?
Don't you remember all the stories
about how I brought you into this beautiful country?
You want to know how to worship me?
You want to know what kind of things
you should give to me?
I don't need your big parties
with so much good food to eat.
And I don't really care if you can sing loudly,
or if you can say many long prayers.
I've already told you what is good.
This is what I want you to do for me.
I want you to be kind and fair to everyone.
I want *everyone*, not just a few,
to have enough to eat.
You don't need to talk loud and sing many songs.
Just quietly, in every little thing you do,
try to live in God's way.'"

Jesus Teaches

BASED ON MATTHEW 5:1–10

Jesus went to many different places to tell people about God's love. People came from everywhere to hear him teach.

Sometimes big crowds of people came. They followed Jesus wherever he went.

But sometimes Jesus just wanted to talk to his special friends, his disciples.

Here are some of the things Jesus said to them about growing in God's way.

If you feel very small inside,
be happy.
God's love is yours.

If you feel very sad inside,
be happy.
God will help you feel better.

If you think you are not very smart,
be happy.
God has a promise for you, too.

If you try very hard to be good,
be happy.

God will help you feel good inside.

If you really care about other people,
be happy.
God cares about you, too.

If you try hard to work for peace,
be happy.
God says, "You are my child."

If people are mean to you because you love God,
be happy.
You will always be part of God's family.

Just Like Salt

BASED ON MATTHEW 5:13–14

Note to leaders: *The shepherd in this story is female. If a child questions this, please explain that in the Middle East most shepherds are women.*

Late one afternoon, Jesus and his friends went for a walk. After a while, they found a shady place to sit down. "I'm hungry," said Andrew. "I brought along some fish and some bread." He passed the basket with the food around to Jesus and his friends.

Just then two shepherds came by. One of them was carrying a wounded lamb. "What happened to your lamb?" asked Andrew. "It looks as if its leg is broken."

"It wandered away from the flock," said the shepherd. "We just found it. The poor thing fell into a hole."

"Do you know how to fix the lamb's leg?" asked Andrew.

The shepherd shook her head. "It's going to be dark soon. It's too late to take it into the town tonight."

"I can fix it," said Andrew. "I need two small sticks to make a splint, and something to make a bandage for the leg."

Peter jumped up and cut some small sticks from a bush. Mary took part of her skirt and tore it into strips for a bandage.

Then Andrew put the sticks against the lamb's leg and wrapped it with the bandage. "Now the lamb's leg will heal so it can walk again."

"Thank you so much!" said the shepherds.

"No problem," said Andrew. "Why don't you stay for a while? Are you hungry? We were just having something to eat."

"Thank you, but no," said one of the shepherds. "Our friends are with the rest of the flock over on that hill. They will worry if we don't get back soon. Thanks again. People like you are the salt of the earth!"

They all waved at the shepherds as they walked toward the hill. "I hope the lamb will be all right!" called Andrew. Then he passed around some more of the bread and fish. They all sat quietly for a while as they ate.

Mary of Magdala looked at Jesus. "We want to live God's way, Jesus, just like you've always said. But I don't really know what that means."

Jesus had been eating a piece of fish. "Andrew," he said, "do you have any salt to put on this fish?" Andrew smiled and handed Jesus a tiny bag with salt in it.

Jesus sprinkled some of the salt on his fish. "Living God's way is a little bit like this salt."

"Like salt?" Mary made a funny face. "How can living God's way be like salt?"

"When I put salt on this fish," said Jesus, "it tastes better. It has more flavour. When you know, deep inside, that God loves you, and then you try to live God's way, that's being like salt. It means that your life has more flavour. It feels good to be alive.

"What is even more important," said Jesus "is that you help make life better for others. The way you did for that lamb and the shepherd. Remember? She said to you, 'You are the salt of the earth.' You are like salt for your family, for your friends, and for lots of people you don't even know. You do things that give their lives more flavour."

By this time it was getting dark. "We're sitting on a nice soft patch of grass," said Andrew. "Why don't we just stay here, rather than walk home in the dark?"

"I have a small oil lamp in my basket," said Mary. "But I don't have any way to light it."

"Look," said Peter, "over there on that hill. The shepherds have a campfire. Give me the lamp. I'll go and ask them to let me light it from their fire."

"Mary," said Jesus, "a few minutes ago you asked about living God's way. And I said it was a bit like being 'salt.'"

Mary laughed a little. "I still think being like salt is kind of funny."

"Well, here's another way to think about living God's way. It's like being a light. Those shepherds have a fire. People can see it from far away. They will light our lamp for Peter, and that will give us light, too."

They all sat quietly for a while as they watched the stars come out in the sky. Then they saw Peter coming back with the glowing lamp. He set it on the ground beside Mary.

"Why don't you put the lamp up on this rock," said Jesus. "That way it will give light to all of us."

"Living God's way is like being a light," said Mary. "We hold our light up high so we can give light to other people, too."

Jesus gave Mary a big smile. "Let's get some sleep," he said. "This grass is nice and soft to sleep on."

The Things Jesus Taught

BASED ON MATTHEW 5:21–37

Note to leaders: *This is the first of four stories all based on the teachings of Jesus, as recorded in Matthew, chapters 5 to 7.*

People often came to Jesus and asked him, "Will you teach us how to live God's way?" Here are some of the things Jesus taught them.

For a long time, your parents, your grandparents, your great-grandparents have known that it is wrong to kill another person. There is never a good reason to kill someone. It is called murder.

Now I want to tell you something harder. If you are angry and you think that you would like to kill someone, that is just as bad. You are murdering that person in your heart.

Don't say things that hurt somebody else. It is wrong to say something that will make them feel bad. It is also harmful if you think mean things about someone. Even if you don't say it out loud.

Sometimes you bring money to the church. That's good. But if you are angry at someone, put the money back into your pocket. Go and talk to that person. Try to become friends again. When you've done that, then you can bring your money to the church.

Never say what you don't mean. When you tell a friend that you will do something, be sure you do it. Don't say, "I forgot," or "I didn't really mean it."

When you make a promise, keep that promise!

Building a Good Strong House

BASED ON 1 CORINTHIANS 3:10–11, 16–23

Paul was worried about his friends who lived in a city called Corinth. They were arguing with each other.

Paul had been to Corinth to tell the people about Jesus. He was the first one to do that. But other people, such as Peter and Apollos, had been there too, and had told the people about living God's way.

Now the people in the church at Corinth were arguing. Some were saying, "Paul is our leader." Others said, "No, Peter is our leader." Still others said, "No. You are both wrong. Apollos is our leader!"

So Paul wrote a letter to the church in Corinth. Here is what he said.

"Please don't argue with each other. Don't argue about who is your leader. Think of it this way. It's like building a house.

"I was the first one to come and tell you about Jesus. I helped you make the bottom part of your house. That's called the foundation. I helped you make it good and strong.

"Then Peter came and told you some more stories. He helped you put nice rooms on top of the foundation of your house.

"And then Apollos came. He told you still more stories. He helped you put a strong roof on your house.

"Every house needs a good foundation so it won't sink into the ground. It needs some rooms so you can live in it. And it needs a roof to keep the rain out. But it's all one house. You need all three parts of it.

"So don't argue about who your leader is. Your little church is like a good house. Peter, Apollos, and I all helped you build it.

"Now live in your house and make it strong."

Change Your Enemy into a Friend

BASED ON MATTHEW 5:38–48

Note to leaders: *This is the second of four stories all based on the teachings of Jesus, as recorded in Matthew, chapters 5 to 7.*

One day when Jesus was playing with some children, a boy and a girl started to get angry at each other.

"You pushed me!" said James.

"I did not," said Susanna. "Stop being so stupid."

"I'm not stupid! You're stupid!"

"Oh yeah?" yelled Susanna. "I'm going to punch you in the nose."

"Wait a minute," said Jesus. "What's happening here?"

"She pushed me and then she called me 'stupid,'" said James.

"Well, he was being stupid," said Susanna.

"What do you feel like doing right now?" Jesus asked Susanna.

"I feel like punching him in the face."

Then Jesus said to James, "If she punched you in the face, what would you do?"

"I'd punch her right back."

"Now if he punched you back," Jesus asked Susanna, "what would you do?"

"I'd punch him back again."

"When you were finished punching each other back and forth, how would you feel?"

Susanna hung her head and James started to cry. They knew what Jesus meant. If they kept punching each other back and forth, they would both have punched-up faces. And they'd still be angry at each other.

"So why don't we try another way?" said Jesus. "Let's start this story all over again, right from the beginning. What happened that started all this?"

"She pushed me," said the James.

"And you yelled at her, right?"

James nodded.

"And she yelled back. So instead of yelling at each other, what could you have done?"

"I don't know," said James.

"Think hard," said Jesus.

"I guess I could have said, 'Please don't push me.'"

Then Jesus turned to Susanna. "When James yelled, 'You pushed me!' what did you do?"

"I yelled back at him."

"What else could you have done?"

"I guess I could have said, 'I'm sorry!'"

"Now, James. If Susanna had said, 'I'm sorry!' instead of yelling back, what could you have done?"

"I could have said, 'That's okay.'"

"If that had happened, maybe you'd still be friends, right?"

Susanna and James nodded.

"Well," said Jesus, "could you pretend that's what happened and be friends again?"

Susanna raised her head and smiled at James, and he smiled back at her.

God Is Like a Loving Mother

BASED ON ISAIAH 49:14–15

It is not easy to live in God's way. Sometimes it is very hard.

Sometimes you may feel that God has forgotten you. Sometimes you may feel that God is very far away. That can make you very sad. It can make you feel afraid.

The prophet Isaiah wrote a book to help us when we feel that way. You can find that book in your Bible.

Here are some of the things he wrote.

God can never forget you.
God is like a loving mother.
Could a loving mother forget her child?
No, of course not.
God is like a woman who is pregnant.
She has a baby growing inside her.
Could she forget about that baby?
No, of course not.
So when you feel God is far away,
remember that God is like a loving mother.

EIGHTH SUNDAY AFTER EPIPHANY

Stop Worrying, Start Thinking

BASED ON MATTHEW 6:24–34

Note to leaders: This is the third of four stories all based on the teachings of Jesus, as recorded in Matthew, chapters 5 to 7.

It was springtime. Flowers bloomed in every field. Birds sang in every tree.

All morning, Jesus had been talking to people who came from many places. They wanted Jesus to tell them how to live God's way.

Then Jesus and his friends sat down under a tree. They were hungry for some lunch. There was bread, cheese, fish, and some water to drink. "Is there any more cheese?" asked Andrew. "I'm still hungry."

"No," said Peter. "We ate all the food. We don't have anything left to eat to-night."

"What are we going to do?" asked Mary. "I could hardly sleep last night. I kept worrying about how we were going to find more food."

"Me, too," said James. "Our money is gone. Now our food is gone, too. I worried all night. What are we going to do?"

"Well," said Jesus, "the first thing we're going to do is stop worrying. I know it's scary not having any food left or money to buy anything."

"How can you say that?" Mary asked. "This is serious!"

"Yes, it is, Mary," said Jesus. "It *is* serious. But take a look around you on this beautiful spring day. Look at all the flowers blooming. Even King Solomon, who had all kinds of money and many fancy clothes – even King Solomon didn't look as nice as these flowers.

"Look at the birds. They fly around and sing. They don't plant seeds to grow food. They don't have any money."

"God cares for these birds and these flowers. God cares even more about you. So stop worrying."

"But we can't just lie down and expect that God is going to drop food out of the sky for us. I mean, get real, Jesus!"

"Yes, get real!" Jesus laughed. "Fussing and worrying isn't going to get us any food. Instead, let's put our heads together. Maybe we can come up with some ideas."

After talking about many different ways to get money to buy food, Susanna had an idea. "I have some rings and earrings at home. I can sell them. Then we'll have money for food."

"But Susanna," said Mary, "I thought you promised your husband that you wouldn't sell your precious things if you travelled with Jesus."

"I did," said Susanna, "but I'll just have to tell him that it's more important to have money so Jesus can keep on teaching people. I made a promise to my husband. I'll keep it if he says 'no.' But he's a good and a kind man. I think he'll understand."

How to Build a Strong House

BASED ON MATTHEW 7:21–29

Note to leaders: This is the fourth of four stories all based on the teachings of Jesus, as recorded in Matthew, chapters 5 to 7.

This is a story Jesus told to his friends.

Living God's way is a bit like building a house.

There was once a man named Jotham. "I am going to build the best house ever," said Jotham. "It's going to be big and strong and everybody will say, 'That's a great house!'"

Jotham often talked about living God's way. He told his friends how he was going to help people when they were sick or hurting or unhappy. But Jotham never really did that. He never went to help anyone.

When someone was telling stories about living God's way, Jotham said he was too busy to listen.

Jotham built his house down on the sand, right beside the water. "Who wants a house way up high on a rock?" he said. "I want my house on the sand so I can run out the front door and go for a swim."

Jotham didn't build his house carefully. Not the way he said he would build it. Instead of using stones for the walls, he used some reeds. Then he just plopped the roof on without tying it down. "I'll do that some other day," he said. "I'm tired."

So when a big storm came and the wind blew really hard, Jotham's house fell down. Crash! That was just the way things happened in his life. He never really tried to live God's way. So when bad things happened in his life, Jotham didn't know that God loved him.

Poor Jotham felt as if he was all alone.

Jotham had a friend named Michael. Michael found a big, solid rock to build his house on. He used good strong stones for the walls. He made sure the roof was tied down really tight.

Michael didn't talk much about building a good, strong house. But that's the kind of house he built.

Michael didn't just talk about living God's way. That's the kind of life he lived. He tried to help other people. When someone was sick or hurting or unhappy,

Michael always went to help. He liked to hear stories about how other people had learned how to live God's way.

One day there was a big storm. The wind blew very hard. But Michael's house didn't fall down.

When some bad things happened in Michael's life, he felt bad and he cried sometimes.

But no matter what happened, Michael always knew that God loved him, and that helped him feel strong inside.

Moses Goes to Visit God

BASED ON EXODUS 24:12–18 AND 31:18

Note to leaders: Another version of this story may be found on page 213.

This is a story that was told a long, long time ago. At first, the story wasn't written on a paper or a stone or on anything else. People just told the story to each other. Moms and dads would tell the stories to their children.

There are many stories in the Bible that were told, from one person to another, long before they were written down. Like this really old story about Moses.

Sometimes the people telling the stories didn't remember them exactly. So the stories changed a little as the older people told them to younger people.

That's why nobody knows for sure whether things happened in just this way. But they kept telling the story, because it helped them remember how wonderful God is. It helped them remember that God really cares about them.

Moses thought he heard a voice. He thought he could hear the voice coming from the top of Mount Sinai. Moses was sure it was God's voice. "Come up to me, Moses. Come right up to the top of this high mountain. If you come up here, I will give you some tablets of stone. They have writing on them. The writing tells you how to live God's way."

Moses was afraid to go alone up to the top of Mount Sinai to visit God. So he asked his friend Joshua to go with him.

But the people of Israel were afraid to be left alone. That's because Moses and Joshua were leaders. They helped people decide what to do. They helped when there was an argument, or if some of the people started fighting. "What will we do while you are gone?" they asked.

"Here is my brother, Aaron," said Moses. "And here is my friend, Hur. If you have a problem, you can talk to them. They will help you decide what to do."

Then Moses and Joshua went up Mount Sinai. But they couldn't get to the top, because for six days there was a big, dark cloud that covered the mountain. Then they heard God's voice again. It sounded like thunder. And they were sure God was there because they could see a big fire in the middle of the cloud.

Moses told Joshua to wait for him. "I am going into the cloud alone," he said. Moses was in the cloud for a long, long time. And while he was there, Moses talked to God, who told him many, many things.

Then God gave Moses two tablets of stone. The tablets had many important things written on them. They told people all the things they should do, and all the things they should not do if they wanted to live God's way.

So Moses brought the tablets down from Mount Sinai and gave them to the people of Israel.

Jesus on the Mountaintop

BASED ON MATTHEW 17:1–9

Note to leaders: *"Nicodemus Comes to See Jesus," based on John 3:1–21, is also a suggested reading for this Sunday and may be found on page 82.*

"What happened, Peter?" Mark asked.

"I can't tell you. Not now," Peter answered.

"Are you sick? You and James and John. You look so pale!"

"No, we're not sick, Mark." Peter was shaking a little. "Something wonderful happened. But I can't tell you about it. Not now."

Years after Jesus was killed and came back to life, Peter finally told the story.

"Jesus took us to the top of a mountain," said Peter. "It was a long climb. We were tired when we got there."

"Just you and Jesus?" Mark asked.

"No, James and his brother John were there, too. They know what happened," said Peter. "I'll never forget that time. All of a sudden, Jesus changed. His face shone. It was like looking into the sun. And his clothes turned white. Really white. Then there were two people with Jesus."

"Who?" Mark asked.

"Elijah and Moses."

"How did you know?"

"I don't know how we knew," said Peter. "But we knew. And Jesus was talking to them."

"So what did you do?" said Mark.

"I didn't know what to do. I said to Jesus, 'Shouldn't we build three little houses here? I could build one for you, one for Moses, and one for Elijah.' It sounds silly now that I think about. But I was so afraid. I didn't know what to say!"

"What did Jesus say?" Mark asked.

"He didn't say anything. A bright cloud came and covered him. Then we heard a voice. James and John heard it, too. You can ask them."

"Was it God?"

"It must have been. The voice said, 'This is my Son. I love him. Listen to him.'"

"That's all?" asked Mark.

"That's all!"

"What did you do?"

"We were so scared. We fell flat on our faces. But then we heard Jesus saying very gently, 'Don't be afraid. Get up.'"

Mark was shaking his head. "I don't understand. Every time I think I understand, I hear something new. Then I have to think about it all over again."

"Yeah!" said Peter. "I know what you mean."

God's Beautiful Garden

BASED ON GENESIS 2:4 – 3:24

This is a story people told many years ago. The story helped them understand why people wear clothes, why some things hurt, and why people have to work.

When God first made the world, there was nothing growing on it. It was all bare. Just soil and rocks and water.

Then God made people. God took some earth. God made it into the shape of a person. Then God breathed gently into it. And the lump of earth became a living person.

God first made two people, a man called Adam and a woman called Eve.

God gave Adam and Eve a very beautiful garden to live in. It was called the Garden of Eden. Eve and Adam walked around naked. God had given them both beautiful bodies, and they didn't mind not having any clothes to wear.

God told Eve and Adam they could eat any of the delicious fruit on the trees, or anything else that grew in the garden.

Except for one tree. God told them not to eat from one special tree, a tree that was right in the middle of the garden.

Now there was a snake in this beautiful garden. The snake liked to make trouble. So one day the snake said to Eve, "Go ahead. Eat the fruit from that special tree. It won't hurt you. Go ahead."

So Eve did. She took some of the fruit, even though she knew she shouldn't. Eve gave some of the fruit to Adam. He ate it too, even though he knew he shouldn't.

As soon as Adam and Eve had eaten the fruit of that special tree, they felt very bad. They felt guilty. So they tried to hide.

Then God came to the garden, and called out, "Where are you?"

Adam was afraid. "I'm hiding here in the bushes because I don't have any clothes on."

God felt sad. God knew that Adam and Eve had eaten the fruit of that special tree. That fruit made them think there was something wrong with the beautiful bodies God had given them.

So God said to Adam and Eve, "You must leave my beautiful garden. Because you didn't do what I asked you to do, things will be harder for you. Your work will sometimes be hard. You will have to grow your own food to eat. And some of the things you have to do will hurt. You will feel pain sometimes and you will cry."

Then God made them some clothes out of animal skins, and told Adam and Eve to leave the beautiful Garden of Eden.

Jesus Gets Ready

BASED ON MATTHEW 4:1–11

"How can I show people how to live in God's way?" Jesus wondered.

Jesus went out into the desert. He found a lonely place where he could think for a long time. Jesus didn't eat any food and drank just a little water. Jesus felt that being very hungry and thirsty might help him hear God.

But for a while, Jesus didn't seem to be hearing God at all. Jesus began to hear an evil voice inside him. The voice talked about the wrong way to be the Messiah. The Messiah was the one who would show everyone what God is like. "Look," said the voice inside Jesus. "Here's an easy way to be the Messiah. Turn those stones into bread. If you give people lots to eat, they will say you are the Messiah."

"No," said Jesus. "The scriptures have told us people need more than bread. They need God's love."

"Well then," said the voice. "Go to the top of the high temple. Jump off. God will help you. You won't hurt yourself. Then everyone will say you are the Messiah."

"No," said Jesus. "The scriptures have told us. Don't try to test God."

"Well then," said the voice. "Go to the top of a mountain. I'll show you all the hills and valleys. I'll show you all the cities and towns. You can be boss of everything if you worship me instead of God. Then everyone will say you are the Messiah."

"No!" said Jesus. "The scriptures have told us serve only God. Don't serve anyone else."

"Bah!" said the voice. "I'll get you later."

Jesus was weak from not having any food. He was tired from all the thinking and praying he had done. Jesus knew that being the Messiah would be very hard.

But he felt strong inside. Jesus knew God had been with him there in the desert. God had helped Jesus choose the right way. Now Jesus was ready to show people how to grow in God's way.

Abraham and Sarah Begin a Journey

BASED ON GENESIS 12:1–4

People in many parts of the world think of Abraham and Sarah as their ancestors. Ancestors are like grandparents. Except you'd have to call them great, great, great – you'd have to say "great" a thousand times – grandparents. Jewish people, Muslim people, and Christian people all think of Abraham and Sarah in this way.

The stories about Abraham and Sarah are very, very old. All the things they did take many stories to tell.

At first their names weren't Abraham and Sarah at all. They were Abram and Sarai, which doesn't sound much different. But for people in Bible times, names were very important.

Abram and Sarai lived in a city called Haran. They liked living there. One day they had a big surprise.

God told Abram and Sarai to move. Just like that.

"Go away from your mother and father. Go away from all the nice things you have in Haran. Just go. I'll tell you where later."

That was a hard thing to do. But Abram and Sarai loved God very much, so they went.

Their nephew Lot went with them. Sarai and Abram were quite rich. They took all their cows and their sheep and their tents. They took many people to help them care for all their animals and things.

Nicodemus Comes to See Jesus

BASED ON JOHN 3:1–21

Nicodemus was an important man. Late one night, when it was very dark, he came to see Jesus. Nicodemus had heard stories about things Jesus had said and done.

Nicodemus wanted his visit to be a secret. He was afraid people might laugh at him.

"Teacher," Nicodemus said to Jesus, "we know that God has sent you. Nobody could do all those wonderful things unless God had sent them."

Jesus looked right at Nicodemus. "Listen to me," he said. "If you really want to grow in God's way, you must be born again."

"But I'm a grownup," said Nicodemus. "I can't go back inside my mother's tummy and be born again!"

"That's not what I mean," said Jesus. "You must become a new person. You must let God's spirit get inside of you. Don't be surprised when I say you must be born again. When people are growing in God's way, they feel brand new, like a tiny baby."

Nicodemus looked puzzled. Sometimes it was hard to understand what Jesus meant.

"God's spirit is like the wind," said Jesus. "You can't see it. But you can see the things the wind does. You won't look any different if you let God's spirit grow inside of you. But you will feel different. And you will care much more about people."

Poor Nicodemus. He tried hard to understand.

"Think of God another way," said Jesus. "Think about God as light. When the light of God shines on things, you can see them in a new way.

"Some people don't like that. They like it better when no one sees the ugly things they do. But if you want to grow in God's way, God's light helps you see. You can clear out the ugly things in your life and bring in things that are clean and bright."

"I get it," said Nicodemus. "When I'm growing in God's way, I'm clean and bright deep down inside. And nobody knows but me."

Jesus smiled. "God knows," he said. "And others will know because you will be a new kind of person."

The Woman at the Well

BASED ON JOHN 4:5–30, 39–42

In the country where Jesus lived, the people were called Jews. A country nearby was called Samaria. The people who lived there were called Samaritans.

"Those Samaritans are lazy and stupid," some of the Jews said. Often the Jews were mean to the Samaritans.

Many people also thought women were not as good as men. "Women should work hard, have babies, and keep quiet," some of the men said. Most of the men wouldn't even talk to a woman. Sometimes they were mean to women.

That's why this story is important. It shows that Jesus doesn't care whether we are boys or girls, whether we are rich or poor. Jesus doesn't care if we are Jews or Samaritans. He doesn't care about the colour of our skin. He doesn't care if we are fat or skinny. Jesus loves everybody.

One day Jesus was walking through the country called Samaria. He was hot and tired, so he sat down to rest by an old well.

Jesus knew about that old well. People called it Jacob's well. Many years ago, the well had been used by Jacob and Rachel and Leah. It reminded Jesus of God's promise to Jacob and Rachel and Leah. God promised to love them and be with them always.

While Jesus was thinking about these things, a Samaritan woman came to the well to get some water. "May I have a drink, too?" Jesus asked the woman.

"What? You are a Jew," she said. "I am a woman and a Samaritan. How come you are talking to me?"

Jesus smiled at her. "If you asked me, I could give you a drink of living water."

The woman laughed. "How can you give me living water?" she asked. "You don't even have a cup or anything to get water from the well."

"If you drink from this well," said Jesus, "you will be thirsty again after a while. If you drink the water I give you, you will never be thirsty again."

The woman understood. Jesus was talking about God's spirit. When God's spirit comes into you, it's like a drink of fresh, cool water.

"Please, give me some of this living water," the woman asked Jesus.

Jesus and the woman had a good talk together. They talked about Jews and Samaritans and about the many ways people worship God.

After a while, Jesus' friends came by. They had gone into the town to buy some food.

Jesus' friends were very surprised to see Jesus talking to a woman. Especially a Samaritan woman. But they didn't say anything.

The woman was so excited about her new friend. She ran into her town and told all the people what happened. They invited Jesus to come and stay with them.

Jesus stayed for two days. He talked with the Samaritans about God. Jesus reminded them that God's promise was for Jews, and for Samaritans, and for everyone. Jesus helped them grow in God's way.

Jesus Heals a Blind Man

BASED ON JOHN 9:1–41

Note to leaders: *Psalm 23 is one of the lectionary readings for this Sunday. You will find it at the Fourth Sunday of Easter, page 105.*

One day, Jesus and his friends were walking through the city of Jerusalem. They met a man who was blind.

Jesus walked over and took the blind man's hand. "What is your name?" he asked.

"Clopas," said the man.

"How long have you been blind?" asked Jesus.

"I haven't been able to see anything my whole life," the man replied.

"Jesus," said one of his disciples, "if Clopas has been blind all his life, it must mean that he did something bad. Or did God make him blind because his mother and father did something bad?"

"No!" Jesus sounded a little bit angry. "God did not make him blind! Clopas didn't do anything bad. Neither did his parents. God doesn't do things like that to people."

Then Jesus turned to Clopas. "Would you like to be able to see?"

"Yes! Yes! Oh yes, I would, please!"

Then Jesus took some of the soil from the ground. He spit on it and mixed it into a little bit of mud. Then he put the mud on Clopas' eyes. "Now," said Jesus, "go and wash your eyes at the Siloam pool. It's not very far from here."

"I know where it is!" Clopas knew how to find his way to lots of places, even though he was blind. He went right to the pool and washed his eyes very clean. Then he jumped up. "I can see! I can see!"

Clopas was dancing around the street he was so glad. So excited. His friends hardly recognized him.

"Are you really Clopas? Are you the man who used to be blind?"

"I sure am!" smiled Clopas.

"How come you can see now?"

"A man named Jesus came. He made a little bit of mud. He put the mud on my eyes and told me to wash it off in the pool. So I did that, and look! I can see!"

"Come," said the friends. "We want to take you to our rulers. They will want to see this."

The rulers were not happy to hear what had happened to Clopas. "I don't believe this," said one of the rulers. "You were never blind. Blind people can never see again, and that's that!"

So the rulers went to see Clopas' mom and dad. "Is this really your son? Is he the one who was born blind? How come he can see?"

"Clopas is our son. That's for sure. He was born blind, but now he can see."

"How could this happen?" asked the rulers.

"How do I know?" said his mom. "Go ask him."

The rulers were getting pretty grumpy. They were afraid people might like Jesus better than them. "People will start to follow Jesus and do what he says," they said to each other. "They might not follow us anymore."

So they went back to Clopas. "We know that Jesus is a bad person," they said. "How come he was able to help you see?"

This time Clopas just danced around. "I already told you what happened. Why do you want me to tell you again? Do you want to become friends of Jesus, too?"

The rulers didn't like that. "We are the rulers. People should follow us. Who is this man Jesus? We don't think he is a good person."

"Isn't that a funny joke?" said Clopas. "He helped me see! God doesn't let bad people do such wonderful things. But when good people pray, God helps them do nice things for others. Jesus is a good man. Jesus helped me see!"

Lazarus Is Alive!

BASED ON JOHN 11:1–53

One of Jesus' best friends had died. His name was Lazarus. Lazarus was the brother of Martha and Mary. They lived in a town called Bethany, where Jesus often visited.

"Oh, Jesus," cried Martha. "If you had been here, my brother wouldn't have died. You could have helped him."

"Mary. Martha," said Jesus. "Try to believe this. Lazarus will live again."

"We all go to live with God when we die," said Martha.

"That's true, Martha," said Jesus. "We all go to live with God when we die. But that's not what I meant. Show me where you buried Lazarus."

So Martha and Mary took Jesus to the grave where they had put Lazarus' dead body. A crowd of people had gathered around.

Jesus cried. His friend was dead.

"Jesus must have loved Lazarus very much," some of the people said.

"Open up the grave," said Jesus. "Take the big stone away from it."

"But he's been dead for four days," said Martha. "His body will smell."

Even so, they took the stone away from the grave.

Jesus prayed. Jesus prayed hard to God. "Please hear me, God," he said.

Then Jesus called with a loud voice, "Lazarus. Come out of the grave!"

"Ooohhh!" everyone gasped. Out of the grave came Lazarus. He had been dead, but now he was alive.

"Give him some clean clothes to put on," said Jesus.

Some of the people in the crowd were not happy to see Lazarus alive again. They were the Pharisees, the rulers.

"Look at that," they said to each other. "Now all the people will do what Jesus tells them. If people follow Jesus, we won't be as important anymore. Maybe we should try to kill Jesus."

Jesus Gets Ready to Die

BASED ON MATTHEW 21:1–11 AND 26:14 – 27:56

There are many stories about Jesus. The most important ones are about how he died and how he came to be with us again in a new and very special way.

Just before he was killed, Jesus tried very hard to show his friends how to live God's way. His friends tried really hard to remember all the things that had happened.

When people try to remember things that happened to them, they forget some parts. That happened with the friends of Jesus, who became the Christian church. People remembered different parts of the story, and often they didn't remember things in quite the same way.

"Let's write the story down before we all forget it!" someone said. So Matthew, Mark, Luke, and John wrote down the stories they had heard about Jesus. They each remembered parts of the story differently. So they each wrote the story of Jesus, but none of the stories were exactly the same.

Here's one story about what happened to Jesus just before he was killed. This is the way it was told by Matthew.

Jesus goes to Jerusalem

"Have you heard about Jesus?" people were saying. "Have you heard about the things he says and does? Everybody knows Jesus!"

Jesus was becoming very famous. Crowds of people came to see him wherever he went. Some people began to wonder, "Is Jesus the Messiah? Is this the leader God promised us?"

Some people thought the Messiah would be like an army general. The Messiah would gather soldiers and fight the Romans. The Messiah would kill the people they didn't like.

Some of Jesus' disciples were also sure Jesus was the Messiah. Even Peter sometimes thought the Messiah would be like a strong soldier in the army.

"I am going to go into Jerusalem," Jesus said to his disciples. "I want you to find me a donkey. I want to ride it into the city."

"A donkey? Why not a big, strong horse?" the disciples asked.

"No, a donkey," replied Jesus. "A small, young donkey. I don't want to go into Jerusalem like a soldier on a horse. If I ride on a donkey, people will know that I am coming to bring peace. I don't want to start a war!"

Soon everyone heard that Jesus was coming. They gathered on both sides of the road. They cheered and shouted as Jesus rode by. Some of them threw down their clothes so the donkey could walk on something soft. Others cut branches from trees for the donkey to walk on.

"Hosanna! Hosanna!" shouted the children.

When the rulers heard the children shouting "Hosanna!" they said to Jesus, "Don't you hear what the children are shouting?"

"Yes," said Jesus. "Of course I can hear them. Don't you know that sometimes children see things – sometimes children know things – even before the adults do?"

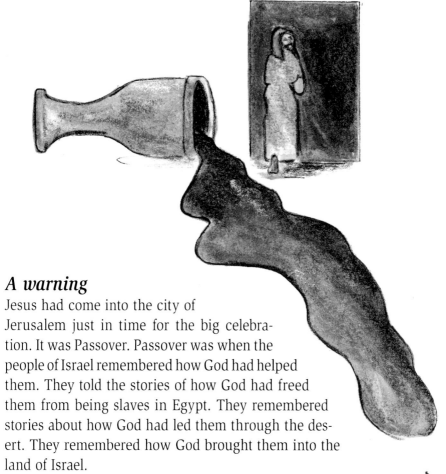

A warning

Jesus had come into the city of
Jerusalem just in time for the big celebration. It was Passover. Passover was when the
people of Israel remembered how God had helped
them. They told the stories of how God had freed
them from being slaves in Egypt. They remembered
stories about how God had led them through the desert. They remembered how God brought them into the
land of Israel.

That night, Jesus and his friends got together for the Passover.
They thought it would be a happy time. And it was. At first.

Then Jesus said something they could hardly believe.

"One of you has stopped being my friend," Jesus told them.
"One of you will show the soldiers who I am so they can arrest
me."

"But who would do this?" asked one of the disciples.

"The one that I give this piece of bread to," said Jesus.

Jesus gave the bread to Judas.

Judas stood straight up. He looked right at Jesus. "You mean I
am going to do this to you?" he asked.

"Yes, Judas, it is you."

Judas rushed out of the room.

For a long time, nobody said a word. Then Jesus spoke. "Something is going
to happen tonight," said Jesus. "Some of you will say you are not my friends."

"Oh no!" said Peter. "Even if everyone else says that, I will always say that I
am your friend."

"Peter," said Jesus. "Before the rooster crows in the morning, you will tell people, 'I am not his friend.' You will do that three times."

"Never," said Peter. "I would rather die first."

Peter is afraid

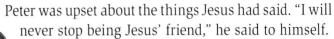

Peter was upset about the things Jesus had said. "I will never stop being Jesus' friend," he said to himself.

That night, the soldiers came. They took Jesus away. Peter ran away at first, because he was so afraid the soldiers would come after him, too.

But then Peter felt a little braver. He started following the soldiers who had taken Jesus. "I will find a way to save Jesus from the soldiers," he thought.

But he was afraid to try anything.

The soldiers took Jesus into a palace. There they yelled at him and hit him and asked him dumb questions.

Outside of the palace, some people had a campfire. It was very late at night. Peter felt cold. He went to the fire to get warm.

A girl looked at Peter. "Aren't you one of Jesus' friends?" she asked.

"I don't know what you're talking about," said Peter. And he turned his back to the girl.

Then another one of the people looked at Peter. "Hey! You were with Jesus!"

"I don't know him!" shouted Peter.

It was very cold. Peter could see a little bit of light in the sky. It would soon be morning. The people standing around the fire could see each other better.

"Sure is cold out here," Peter said. He was trying to be friendly.

"You talk just like Jesus talks," said one of the men. "You must be one of his friends."

"I am not," Peter screamed. "I don't know him! I've never heard of him! I am not his friend!"

Just then, Peter heard the rooster crow.

Peter remembered!

Peter remembered what Jesus had told him. "Before the rooster crows in the morning, you will say, 'I don't know him!' three times."

Peter ran away from the warm campfire. He felt all cold inside.

And Peter began to cry.

Jesus is killed

The rulers who had taken Jesus away wanted to have him killed. They took Jesus to the man who was in charge of the whole country. His name was Pilate. Only Pilate could have people killed.

"Why do you want me to kill Jesus?" Pilate asked.

"Because Jesus says he is the Messiah," said the rulers. "A Messiah is like a king. If Jesus is a king, then we should obey him instead of you."

"Is that true?" asked Pilate. "Are you the Messiah?"

"Yes, that is true," said Jesus.

"All right!" said Pilate to the rulers. "I'll give the orders to my soldiers. They will take Jesus and kill him.

Then the soldiers took Jesus away. They teased Jesus. They beat him.

The soldiers made a cross. The cross was made of two very thick pieces of wood. And then the soldiers said to Jesus, "You carry your own cross."

After that terrible beating, Jesus could hardly walk. He couldn't carry the heavy wooden cross. The solders grabbed a man called Simon of Cyrene and made him help. Simon had to carry the cross all the way to the garbage dump, a place called Golgotha.

There, the soldiers laid the cross on the ground. They took a big hammer and nailed Jesus to the cross. Then the soldiers raised it up. Jesus hung there by the nails through his hands and his feet. It hurt terribly.

"Hey, you!" the soldiers yelled. "If you're the Messiah, save yourself."

"Yeah," called another. "If you really are God's chosen one, come down off that cross."

It seemed like such a long time that Jesus hung there on the cross. The pain got worse and worse. Most of Jesus' friends had run away. The only ones who stayed were Mary of Magdala and the other women who were Jesus' friends.

All of them were crying.

"My God," Jesus screamed. "My God, why have you left me all alone?"

Then Jesus died.

Mary of Magdala Sees Jesus

BASED ON JOHN 20:1–18

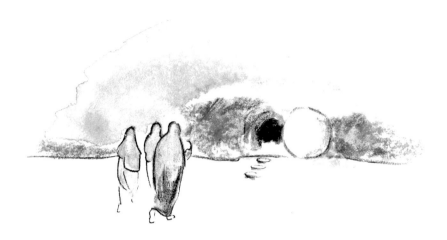

Mary of Magdala had been one of Jesus' friends.

Mary didn't run away when the rulers killed Jesus. She and some of the other women disciples stayed near Jesus all the time that he hung on the cross.

Mary wanted so much to help Jesus. But the soldiers wouldn't let her.

Now Jesus was dead. Mary felt as if she had died, too.

Early on Sunday morning, on the third day after Jesus had been killed, Mary went to the place where they had put Jesus' dead body. But when she got there, she saw that Jesus' body was gone.

Mary was very upset. She ran to call some of Jesus' other disciples. They came running as fast as they could. They, too, saw that Jesus' dead body wasn't there anymore.

Jesus' other disciples didn't know what to do, so they went home. Mary stayed behind. She wanted to be by herself for a while. She wanted to have a good cry. Mary was very sad about all the things that had happened to Jesus.

While she was crying, she looked into the place where they had put Jesus' body. She saw two angels. The angels asked her, "Why are you crying?"

"They have taken Jesus away," said Mary. "And I don't know where they have put him."

Then Mary turned around, and she saw somebody standing there. She was still crying, and the tears in her eyes made it hard for her to see who it was.

"Who are you looking for?" this person asked. "And why are you crying?"

Mary cried even harder. "If you have taken Jesus away, please tell me where you have put him, and I will go and get him."

"Mary," he said.

As soon as she heard her name, she knew who it was.

"Teacher!" she shouted. She was so happy. Jesus had been dead, but now he was alive again!

"Go and tell the other disciples," said Jesus. "Tell them that I am going to live with God."

So Mary of Magdala went running just as fast as she could – running and jumping and shouting because she was so happy.

Jesus was alive again!

SECOND SUNDAY OF EASTER

Thomas Asks Questions

BASED ON JOHN 14:1–7, 20:19–29

"Don't ask so many questions, Thomas."

That's what Thomas' teachers said in school.

That's what Thomas' parents said at home.

That's what Thomas' friends said.

But Thomas couldn't help it. When the Rabbi, the teacher, told them things in school, Thomas often asked, "How do you know?"

Sometimes that made the Rabbi angry. "I know just because I know, Thomas. It is true because I say so."

Thomas had to be quiet, but he didn't like the teacher's answer. Thomas was sad when his questions made people angry. But he couldn't stop asking.

When Thomas grew older, he became one of Jesus' special friends. He became a disciple. Thomas liked Jesus, because Jesus never told him to stop asking questions.

One day Jesus was trying to explain what was going to happen. "I am going away," said Jesus. "I am going to get a place ready for you. God's house has room for you and for everyone else. You know the way to God's house."

"No we don't," said Thomas. "What is the way?"

"That's a good question, Thomas," smiled Jesus. "I am the way. If you really love me, and love each other, then you know the way."

"I still don't understand all of it," said Thomas.

"That's okay," said Jesus. "Just keep asking questions."

Not long after that, Jesus died. He was killed by people who didn't like the way he said that God loved everyone. Thomas was very sad when Jesus was killed, so when some of the other disciples said Jesus was alive again, Thomas really wanted to believe them.

But he couldn't. His mind kept asking questions. "How can somebody be dead and then be alive again?" When some of the disciples told Thomas they had seen Jesus, Thomas asked, "How can you be sure it was Jesus? How do you know it wasn't somebody else?"

"But we saw him with our own eyes," said the disciples.

"Maybe," said Thomas. "But I have to see for myself. I have to see the places in Jesus' hands where they put the nails. Otherwise, I won't believe it."

A few days later, Thomas and his friends were together. All the doors were closed, but suddenly, there was Jesus in the room with them. He smiled at Thomas. "Come here, my friend. Touch the places where they put the nails. It really is me."

Thomas began to cry, he was so happy to see Jesus. "Oh, yes, it is you Jesus. I am so glad. Now I know that you are alive again. I won't ask any more questions."

"Oh, don't stop asking questions, Thomas," said Jesus. "I am glad you are able to see me so you can be sure. Then you can believe. But there will be lots of people who won't be able to see me. They will ask questions, too. It will be hard for them to believe, just as it was hard for you to believe. I will need you to help tell them my story."

"You mean, you're not angry because I didn't believe right away that you were alive again?" Thomas asked.

"No, not angry at all," said Jesus. "I like it when people ask hard questions. But you won't understand everything, Thomas. You will never find answers to all your questions. Just remember that I love you and that God loves you. Nobody can prove that part, but it is the part that is the most true."

On the Road to Emmaus

BASED ON LUKE 24:13–35

"I can't figure it out," said Cleopas. "Peter says Jesus' body is gone. And Mary says she saw Jesus. She says Jesus isn't dead anymore."

"I don't believe that," said the other disciple. "When someone is killed, they are dead. They can't come alive again!"

It was the Sunday after Jesus was killed. The two disciples were walking along the road to a town called Emmaus. As they walked, a stranger came and walked with them. They didn't know who he was.

"What are you talking about?" asked the stranger. "And why are you so sad?"

"Where have you been?" asked Cleopas. "Are you the only one who doesn't know about all the things that happened?"

"What things?" asked the stranger.

"The rulers," said Cleopas. "And the soldiers. They hated Jesus. They killed Jesus."

"Why did they hate Jesus?" the stranger wanted to know.

"Who knows? Maybe they thought Jesus was going to start an army and fight them. Jesus told us he would be killed. Then Jesus said he would come alive again

in three days. That's pretty hard to believe. Anyway, here it is, the third day since he was killed. Mary of Magdala says he's alive, but I don't believe her. As far as we know, Jesus is dead."

Then the stranger began to talk to them. The stranger told the story of Moses and of all the prophets. "Do you find it hard to believe that Jesus was killed?" asked the stranger. "Do you find it hard to believe that he came alive again?"

"Yeah. We sure do," said Cleopas.

The three of them reached the town of Emmaus. "Why don't you come in and stay with us?" they said to the stranger. "It's almost dark outside. Besides, you must be hungry."

Soon they were ready to have a meal together.

Then the stranger took a piece of bread, and broke it. He gave Cleopas and the other disciple pieces of the bread.

Suddenly Cleopas remembered. He remembered the last supper Jesus had with his friends. He remembered how Jesus had broken the bread.

"It's you!" shouted Cleopas. "It's you, Jesus! You're alive!"

And the stranger was gone.

"We should have known," said Cleopas. "When we were walking along. The way he talked to us. I felt warm and good inside as I listened to him. We should have known it was Jesus. We should have believed what Mary told us!"

"Let's go tell the rest of Jesus' friends," said the other disciple. "Let's go to Jerusalem!"

So off they went, hurrying as fast as they could. They found the rest of Jesus' disciples gathered together. "Jesus is alive!" said Cleopas.

"We know," said the disciples. "Simon saw him. Isn't it wonderful?"

"Oh yes!" said Cleopas. Then he told the disciples how he and his friend had walked along the road with a stranger. "We didn't know who he was, until we started to eat. Then we remembered how we ate with Jesus, just before he was killed. It was just at that moment, when he took a loaf of bread and gave it to us to eat. We saw it was Jesus! And then he was gone."

God Is My Shepherd

BASED ON PSALM 23

I think of God as my shepherd
who gives me all that I need;
who lets me lie down,
on soft green grass,
beside a quiet stream.

I think of God as my shepherd,
who helps me do what is right.
God helps me feel strong
when I'm weak and afraid,
when I'm crying
for someone who's sad.

My shepherd is glad when I'm happy,
and gives me good things to eat.
I know I'm invited
to live in God's house
for all the days of my life.

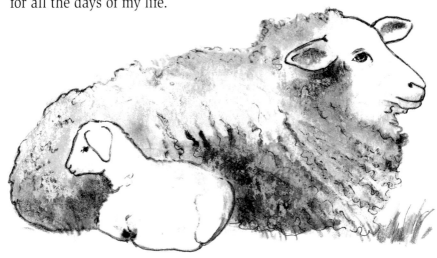

Susanna Has a Good Idea

BASED ON ACTS 2:42–47, AND JOHN 10:1–10

The people who knew Jesus – Mary of Magdala, Susanna, Andrew, and all the others – liked to talk about the things Jesus said before he died.

"Do you remember how Jesus liked to talk about sheep?" Andrew asked.

"It makes me laugh a little when I think about it," said Mary. "Jesus didn't have any sheep, but he liked to call himself a shepherd."

"We are the sheep he looked after," said Andrew.

"I know, and that's why I laugh. Sheep are smelly, and they are not very smart. They keep wandering away from the flock, so they get lost."

"That's why!" said Andrew. "That's why Jesus said we were like sheep. We keep wandering away from the flock."

"But we're not as smelly!" laughed Mary.

"No," laughed Andrew. "I don't think Jesus cared if we were a little bit smelly from being out in the hot sun all day.

"Jesus really wanted us to stay together to help each other live in God's way. Remember how he talked about 'the abundant life'? I think Jesus meant that we should help each other. We should love each other and share with each other. Then we would be really happy."

Susanna was just listening to Mary and Andrew. Susanna didn't talk very much. But when she did talk, she usually said something really important.

"I think I know how Jesus would like us to live God's way," said Susanna. "None of us have much money. But what if we put all our money together – with the other things we have, like our clothes and our houses? What if we said we would share everything with everybody?"

"But you have way more money than I have," said Andrew. "And you have way more nice clothes and other things. Would you want to put that together with the few cheap things I have? And my tiny bit of money?"

"Yes, Andrew!" said Susanna. "We could share what we have. I have more money, but you have stronger muscles. You can help lift things and carry things. Mary knows how to give great hugs when we're feeling sad. Let's each give the things we have."

"Then we'll all be richer, and we'll all be happier." Andrew smiled. "That's a really good idea, Susanna. I think Jesus would like that."

"I think that's what Jesus was talking about," said Mary. "He talked about 'the abundant life.' If we all share what we have, we can all be happier!"

A Letter to the People of the Way

BASED ON 1 PETER 2:2–10

After Jesus had been killed, his friends were very sad. Jesus was dead, for sure. But at other times, somehow, he also seemed to be alive. It wasn't long before they knew that Jesus was still with them. His body was dead. But in some wonderful way, Jesus' friends knew that he lived in their hearts.

They kept remembering the things Jesus did. They talked about the things Jesus said. They told lots of other people about Jesus. They told them what Jesus was like and why they loved him so much.

Soon there were many others who knew that Jesus was still alive. They had never seen Jesus. But they heard stories about him. Soon Jesus was alive in their hearts, too.

People got together to talk about Jesus. Often, they got together in people's homes. "We need to help each other live God's way," they said. They called themselves a "church."

The people in these churches liked to sing songs and pray to God. Sometimes they brought food so they could eat together. "Remember how Jesus liked to eat with his friends?" they said. They called that meal "communion."

The people in the churches knew that living God's way was sometimes very hard. They sent letters to help people in other churches feel stronger and braver.

Here's what one of those letters said.

"Imagine that you are just tiny babies. Newborn babies need to have milk from their mothers, or they will die. Think of God as your mother. God wants to feed you, just like a mother feeds her baby. That's why you sing songs about Jesus. That's why you hear stories about Jesus. That's why you try to help other people be safe and happy.

"When you do those things, God is feeding you like a mother feeds her baby.

"Here's another way you can think about living God's way. Imagine that you are a stone that is part of a building. You put stones one on top of the other, to make a wall. If you pull one stone out of that wall, the whole wall might fall down. Each one of you is like a stone that makes the building strong. Each one of you is important in the church.

"Some people don't like you because you go to a church. They tease you and hurt you. It is hard to live God's way.

"It was hard for Jesus to live God's way, too. People hurt him and they killed him. But God says, 'Jesus is the most important stone. Jesus is the most important part of the church.'

"You are like a very important stone – an important part of God's church. That's why we need you to be as strong as you can. We need you for our church."

A Room in God's House

BASED ON JOHN 13:33 – 14:14

Peter was feeling tired. "Being your friend is like going to school," he said to Jesus. "We have to learn so many things."

Jesus put his hand on Peter's shoulder. "I know, Peter. But I will go away soon, so you need to know these things before I leave."

"Where are you going?" asked Peter.

"I am going to a place where you can't come," said Jesus.

"Why not?" said Peter. He was beginning to feel very sad.

"You can't come with me now," said Jesus, "but you can come later."

Jesus' friends were even more puzzled. They didn't know that Jesus was talking about how he was going to die. They didn't know that he was going to live with God – not here with them.

"Try hard not to worry," said Jesus. "Try to believe that God loves you and that I love you, too. There are many different rooms in God's house, and I'm going to get a room ready for each of you. And not just for you, but for all of God's people."

Thomas was still feeling worried. "How can we follow you? We don't know where you are going!"

"You do know the way, Thomas. You love me. You love God. You love other people. That's the way. It is your love that will take you to God's house."

Philip had an idea. "Jesus. If you can let us see where God lives, then we will know what God is like."

"Take a close look at me, Philip. If you have seen me, and if you have felt the deep love I have for you, then you know what God is like. That's because I am part of God and God is part of me."

"That's really hard to understand," said Philip.

"I know," said Jesus. "So just remember to love God. If you love God, you will love me, and you will love other people. When you love other people, you will love God."

Jesus could see that Philip didn't really understand. "Do you feel mixed up, Philip?"

"Yes, I do." Peter and Thomas were nodding their heads. They were mixed up, too.

"Then just remember this. The way to love God is to be kind and gentle and fair to everyone. Including yourself, too. When you do that, you will be loving God."

The God with No Name

BASED ON ACTS 17:16–31

Paul really wanted everyone to know. "Jesus came to show us how to live God's way," he said.

Paul travelled to many different countries. He told the story of Jesus to anyone who would listen to him.

One day, Paul was in the city of Athens, which is in Greece. He walked around looking at all the interesting things. Paul noticed that there were a lot of statues with names on them: "The God of Thunder," or "The God of War," or "The God of Food." There were many others.

But the sign on one of the statues said, "To the God with no name." Paul wondered why people would have a statue for a god they didn't know.

Whenever Paul saw people standing or sitting together, Paul would talk to them. "Can I tell you about my friend Jesus?" he would ask. "Jesus showed us how to live God's way."

Some of the people just got angry. "Go away! You're a stranger. We don't want to listen to you talk about your God!"

But some of the others said, "What you are saying is interesting. If we get people together, will you come and talk to us? We want to know about your friend Jesus."

Many people gathered. Paul spoke in a loud voice so everybody could hear. "My friends, you live in a beautiful city. As I was walking around, I saw that you have a lot of statues of gods. You have a god of thunder. You have a god of war and a god of food. You have so many different gods.

"Then I saw a statue that said, 'The god with no name.'

"Well, I have a nice surprise for you. I can tell you about that God. The God with no name is the God who made everything. This God made the stars and the moon. This God made the world and everything that's in it. This God even made you and me.

"Do you want to know something else? This God is the only god. Those other gods you made are only statues. They are only pretend gods.

"Here's the best part. I have a friend named Jesus. Jesus came to show us just what God is like. This God is like a parent – like a very loving mother or father. Jesus showed us that this God loves you and me. This God loves every person in the whole world.

"You can never make a statue that looks like God. Even if it's a beautiful statue made of gold and silver, covered with diamonds. If you want to know what God is like, then I will tell you the story of Jesus."

Most of the people of Athens didn't like what Paul told them. "We like our own gods," they said. So they went away.

But some of them stayed. "Tell us more about Jesus," they said. "We want to know how to live God's way."

Jesus' Friends Feel Stronger

BASED ON ACTS 1:6–14 AND LUKE 24:44–53

After Jesus had been killed, his friends were very sad. But then Jesus came back to them. "It doesn't make sense," said Thomas. "How can somebody who is dead be alive?"

For many days nothing happened. They waited and waited for Jesus to come back again. "We want Jesus to come and tell us what to do."

Mary, Jesus' mother, was the saddest of all. "I don't know what to do," she said. "I know Jesus came to show us how to live God's way. We all want to do that. But we don't know how!"

Waiting for Jesus made them very sad. Sad people often need others to help them cry. So Jesus' friends got together. They gave each other hugs. They cried together. They prayed together.

They prayed for God to help them. "Please tell us how to live in God's way," they prayed. "Please help us not feel so sad about Jesus."

Then something happened. Jesus' friends began to feel stronger.

They talked about Jesus. They told each other the stories Jesus had told them. They remembered the things Jesus had done. And the things he said. It almost felt as if Jesus was still there with them.

"You know," said Peter. "I think Jesus is right here with us. If we just wait, maybe something will happen. I think Jesus will come to us again. But in a new way."

"You're right, Peter," said Susanna. "If we stay together, Jesus will come to us."

"Don't be silly," said Thomas. "Jesus is dead. We should stop pretending that he is still alive."

"No, Thomas," said Peter. "I can feel it in my heart. Jesus is right here with us. Right now. But you know something, I think Jesus promised something even more wonderful!"

"Yes," said Susanna. "Yes! Yes! Jesus wants us to stay together. He wants us to pray together. When we do that, Jesus is with us. And Jesus will come back to us with something more."

"That sounds like a riddle," said Thomas. "How do you know that?"

"I don't *know* that, Thomas," said Susanna. "But I *believe* that! I believe that because I remembered what happened not long after Jesus died."

"You mean when Jesus came to us in the upstairs room? We thought he was some kind of a ghost, but it was really Jesus," said Thomas.

"Yes," Peter was really smiling now. "And do you remember his promise, Susanna?"

"I sure do." Susanna was almost laughing, she was smiling so hard. "Jesus said God's Spirit would come to us. The Holy Spirit. And the Holy Spirit would make us strong, and we would know what we should do. I really believe that will happen, Thomas."

"I'm trying to believe it," said Thomas.

Peter put his arm around Thomas' shoulder. "Don't worry Thomas. When it happens, then you'll be able to believe."

The Birthday of the Church

BASED ON ACTS 2

It was seven weeks since Jesus died. But the disciples knew Jesus was still alive.

One day, the disciples were all together, with many other people. It was the day of Pentecost, an important time for Jewish people.

Then something very strange happened. Some said there was the sound of a strong wind. Others said there were little bits of fire dancing around among the disciples.

The strangest part was that the disciples began to talk in new ways. Nobody was sure what kind of languages they spoke. Even the disciples weren't sure about the new words they heard themselves saying.

But others understood. "Hey!" someone said. "I come from a place where we speak a different language. How come I can understand what he's saying?"

People were there from many faraway places. They understood many different languages. Yet they could each understand what the disciples were saying.

"What is going on here?" people asked.

"You drank too much wine!" somebody said to Peter.

"No," said Peter. Then he stood up and talked to all the people who had come together for Pentecost.

"My friends," said Peter, "we're not drunk. Something very important has happened here." Then Peter told them the whole story, beginning many, many years ago with Abraham and Sarah, right up until the time of Jesus. Then Peter told them how Jesus was God's Messiah.

Peter explained that from now on, God's Spirit would be with everyone who believed in Jesus. We would not be able to see Jesus alive again the way the disciples had seen him. But Jesus would be alive in our hearts. Peter called it "the Holy Spirit."

"What should we do?" someone asked.

"Be sorry for the wrong things you have done," said Peter. "Believe that God really loves you."

Many people said, "Yes, we want to do that." So they were baptized in water. Being baptized was a way of saying, "I want to live in God's way."

The disciples were happy. Now they knew what Jesus wanted them to do. Jesus wanted the disciples to help everyone know about God's love.

So the disciples went to many places. They told people about Jesus and about God's promise.

Many people came to the disciples and said, "Yes, I believe that Jesus is God's Messiah. I want to live in God's way."

Soon there were people in many places who knew about Jesus. These people got together to help each other, to eat together, to remember the things that Jesus said, and to talk about living in God's way. When people came together like this, they called it a church.

How to Be a Strong Church

BASED ON 1 CORINTHIANS 12:4–13

The people in the church in a town called Corinth had a problem. "We want to be a strong church that helps us live God's way," they all said. "And we want to tell and show others how to live God's way."

"I know," said Lois. "We have to learn how to cook good food. We have to learn how to talk about God and about the things that Jesus said and did."

"And we have to learn how to sing. We have to learn how to clean up our mess." Timothy made a sour face when he said that. "We have to learn how to help people who are sick."

"Whoops!" said Lois. "We forgot about praying. We *especially* have to learn how to pray and to teach others to pray, because it's most important."

"Wait a minute," said Chloe. She was laughing a little bit. "Don't you remember the letter we got from Paul? He came to our city to tell us the stories about Jesus. And he had a really good suggestion about how to do all those things."

"I kind of remember," said Timothy. "Didn't Paul say something about how the church was like a person's body?"

"Right. The church is like our bodies. We have feet. We have hands. We have noses. We have many different parts and each part does something special."

"So?"

"So, your hand doesn't have to know how to run. And your feet don't have to know how to pick things up. Your nose can't hear anything."

"That's funny," said Lois. "What if your nose could hear things? I would put my nose close to your mouth so I could hear what you are saying."

"And then I would put my ear close to my food so I could smell it," laughed Timothy.

"You might get ketchup in your ear!" giggled Lois.

Chloe was laughing, too. "Each part of your body does one thing best. So in our church, each one of us does one thing best."

"I like to sing," said Timothy.

"Good," said Chloe. "So you work hard to be really good at singing, and then you can help the rest of us sing along with you. What do you do best, Lois?"

"I like to tell stories. I know some good stories."

"And I like to cook," said Chloe. "Now we need to talk to the other people in our church. We need to find out what they like to do best. There are many different things to be done. That's why we like to have many different kinds of people in our church."

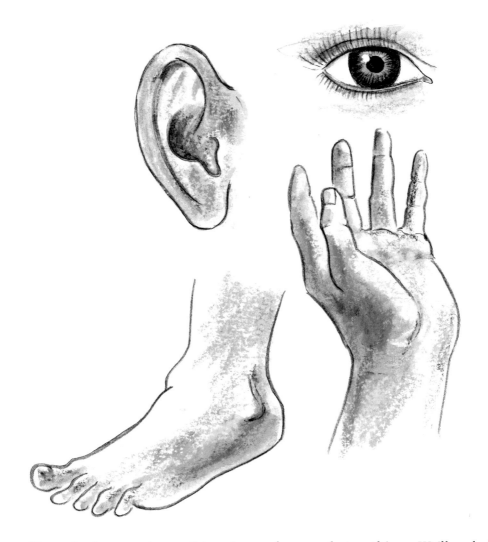

"So each of us can do one thing. Some of us can do two things. We'll each do the things we know how to do. Then we can be a strong church," said Lois.

"That's important," said Chloe. "Paul told us that our church is like our bodies. There are different parts of our body, but every one of them is important. We have arms and legs and eyes and ears. Each part of our body does something different, but we need each part. Our church is like a person's body. Every person in our church helps us be a strong church. Every person is important."

"I don't think anyone will want to be good at cleaning up the mess," said Timothy.

"I don't think so either," laughed Chloe. "So maybe that's one thing we'll all do together."

God Makes a Universe

BASED ON GENESIS 1

This is a story people told many, many years ago. They told this story, because they were trying to understand why God made the world.

Close your eyes very tight. You can't see anything... right? Now let's pretend.

Pretend you can imagine nothing.

That's right. Nothing!

Imagine a long, long time ago when there was no world. No stars. No animals. No people. No you.

Just nothing.

Now imagine that even though there was nothing, God was there.

Before there was anything, there was God.

Because God isn't a "something." God just is.

It's very hard to imagine that, isn't it? But that's the way the Bible tells us it was at the beginning of everything.

God was there. God was there like a strange light that is everywhere, but doesn't come from anywhere. The light didn't shine on anything, because there was nothing to shine on. Can you imagine that?

You can open your eyes now.

God had an idea. "Let there be light!" said God. And it happened! Maybe it was like a really loud whoosh! Scientists call it a "big bang"! A bigger bang than you could ever imagine. A bigger flash of bursting light.

Out of all that nothing, God made something.

Out of that big bang came stars. Gazillions of stars! All the stars you can see in the night sky. You can see even more stars if you look through a telescope.

Some of the stars have planets and moons.

One of the stars that God made was our sun that shines in the sky every day. One of those planets was our earth – the one you live on right now. One of the moons was our moon, the one we see at night.

And God said, "That's good!"

God kept having ideas. God kept making things. Lakes and rivers and oceans. Trees and plants. Animals and bugs. God made things slowly and carefully, and sometimes it took many, many years – more years than you can imagine – to make things. Scientists call that "evolution."

And God said, "That's good!"

Then God said, "I'm going to make people. Each person will be like the animals in many ways. But in one special way, these humans will be like me."

So God made people. People like you. And inside each one of us, God put some of the light that was there before there was anything. You have some of that light in you. People can see that light shining in your eyes when you laugh. Sometimes they also see God's light when you cry. And sometimes they see that light when you are just being you.

And then God looked at all creation. God looked at the stars, the world, the mountains and trees and flowers and bugs. God looked at the animals and the birds. God even looked at things so tiny we can't see them – bacteria and molecules and atoms and protons.

God looked at the people. God looked at the babies and children and adults and old people. God looked at people with dark skins and light skins. God looked at all the many kinds of people.

Then God said to the people, "I'm giving you this beautiful world – this beautiful universe. Please take good care of it. Please be kind to it."

When it was all done, God said, "This is all very good!" And God smiled a smile as wide and beautiful as the rainbow.

A Song from the Bible

BASED ON PSALM 8

God, you are wonderful.
When I think of your love, I feel strong.
You have made the stars in the sky
and you made me – a tiny new baby.

Oh, God, when I look up at the sky,
at the moon and the stars that you made,
I feel so small, so tiny and weak.
Do you care about children?
Do you care about grownups, too?

You made us, God, to be a little like you.
Because of that, we are strong and loving.
You've given us the world to take care of,
all the animals and all the birds,
and everything else in the world.

God, you are wonderful.
When I think of your love, I feel strong.

To try a liturgical dance or movements
to this psalm see page 250.

God Makes a Promise

BASED ON GENESIS 6:1 – 9:17

Note to leaders: *One of the readings for this Sunday is Matthew 7:21–29. A story based on this reading can be found on page 70, the Ninth Sunday after Epiphany.*

Here is a story about a man named Noah and his family.

People many years ago told this story because it helped them understand something called a "covenant."

When people get married, they promise to love each other. They promise to be good to each other. That is a covenant.

Some parents bring a new baby to church. The baby is baptized or dedicated. They say, "God loves us, and we love God." They promise to tell the baby about God's love. The people in the church promise to help them. That is a covenant.

When people come to join the church, they remember God's love. They promise to try their best to live in God's way. That is a covenant.

The long-ago people in the Bible knew that God had promised to be with them always. So they promised to remember God's love. That is a covenant. God's covenant.

The Bible tells us many stories about how people didn't always remember how that covenant got started. They acted as if they didn't care about God.

When that happened, someone would tell the story of Noah. Then they would remember God's covenant with them.

Noah was a very old person. Noah and his wife liked to talk with God. They and their children tried very hard to live in God's way.

It wasn't easy. All the other people in the place where the Noah family lived didn't even think about God. They fought and killed each other. They stole things and told lies. They were mean to each other. It made God very unhappy.

God became so unhappy, God finally decided to start the world all over again with new people.

So God said to Noah and his family, "Build a boat. A special kind of boat called an ark."

Then God told them how to build this ark. "It must be very big. So big that it can hold two of every kind of animal and bird in the world."

The people who didn't listen to God thought Noah was very silly. "There isn't any water anywhere near," they said. "Just dry land. That's stupid, building a boat where there isn't any water!"

Noah and his family knew it looked pretty strange. But God had told them to build this boat, so they were going to build it.

It took a long time to finish the ark. Mr. and Mrs. Noah and all their children worked at it together. When it was finally done, God told the Noah family to find two of every kind of animal and bird.

Two dogs. Two cats. Two horses. Two tigers. Two snakes. Two wallabies. Two bugs. Even two skunks. Two of everything.

It was very noisy and smelly when they had all those animals crowded into that big boat.

"Get in," God said. The Noah family got into that boat with all those animals and birds.

But the ark didn't go anywhere. It just sat there on the dry land.

"Wait," God told them gently. "Just wait."

The people who lived nearby came and laughed at how silly it all looked. Here was this huge boat, full of all those animals, with Noah and his family shut up tight inside. But there was no water. Everything was dry all around.

"Do we have to sit in this awful ark forever?" asked one of Noah's children.

"Try to be patient," said Noah.

But even Noah was finding it hard to be patient.

Then, all of a sudden, it started to rain. It was almost as if God had just opened up the sky, it rained so hard. It kept raining and raining. The people left outside the ark, and all the animals that couldn't come into the ark, all died.

The ark floated up on the water and drifted around. It drifted and drifted and drifted. The Noah family and all the animals and birds in the ark got so tired of just staying in that boat.

"Is this ark just going to float around forever?" asked one of the children.

Inside the ark it was pretty smelly. The animals would sometimes fight with each other. "This place stinks!" said the grandchildren.

Then, one day, the sun came out and the wind began to blow. Noah decided to see if there was dry land anywhere. He wanted to get off that smelly ark as much as anyone.

So Noah took one of the birds, a raven, and let it fly away. But the raven came back very tired. It couldn't find any place to land. There was still water everywhere.

Then Noah tried a dove, and the same thing happened.

So the Noah family waited some more. They waited a whole week. They were getting so tired of waiting.

Then Noah tried the dove again. It flew off, and seemed to stay away a long time. When it came back, it had some olive leaves in its beak.

"Look," yelled Noah. "The dove found some leaves. That means there's some land somewhere."

Everyone cheered and all the children danced around as happy as anything. The Noah family had been on the ark for forty days and forty nights. It felt like such a long time. Now they knew it wouldn't be long before they'd be able to get off the ark and start a new life.

"The first thing we do, when we get off the ark," said Noah, "is to say thank you to God."

As soon as the ark came to some dry ground, everybody got out as quickly as they could.

The Noah family piled up some rocks to make an altar. Then they put some wood on the altar and set it on fire. They put some good food on the fire and hoped the smell of the good food would go up to God. They were sure God would know they were saying "thank you"!

They let all the animals out of the boat. The animals ran around and jumped and smelled the grass and the trees. It looked as if they were saying "thank you" to God in their own way. Everyone was very happy.

God was happy, too.

The Long Journey of Abraham and Sarah

BASED ON GENESIS 12, 13:14–18

People in many parts of the world think of Abraham and Sarah as their ancestors. Ancestors are like grandparents. Except you'd have to call them great, great, great – you'd have to say "great" a thousand times – grandparents. Jewish people, Moslem people and Christian people all think of Abraham and Sarah in this way.

The stories about Abraham and Sarah are very, very old. All the things they did take many stories to tell.

At first their names weren't Abraham and Sarah at all. They were Abram and Sarai, which doesn't sound much different. But for people in Bible times, names were very important.

Abram and Sarai lived in a city called Haran. They liked living there. One day they had a big surprise.

God told Abram and Sarai to move. Just like that.

"Go away from your mother and father. Go away from all the nice things you have in Haran. Just go. Ill tell you where, later."

That was a hard thing to do. But Abram and Sarai loved God very much, so they went.

Their nephew Lot went with them. Sarai and Abram were quite rich. They took all their cows and their sheep and their tents. They took many people to help them care for all their animals and things.

It was like a camping trip with lots of people. Except it probably wasn't very much fun. Abram and Sarai and the rest would walk a long way. Then they would set up all their tents. After a while, they would go somewhere else. Sometimes it was hot. Or dusty. Sometimes they hurt their feet on the sharp stones.

They went to a place called Shechem, where Abram built an altar to offer sacrifices to God.

Then they went to Bethel, then to Ai, then to Negev, and even all the way to Egypt. They just kept travelling and travelling.

When Abram and Sarai would talk to each other at night, just before they went to sleep, they would wonder, "Why doesn't God tell us where we are going?"

Each time, they remembered that when God had said, "Go," God had also made them a promise.

"Your children's children's children's children will be a great nation. People will remember you for years and years. They will remember you and what you have done. People all over the world will learn to live God's way because of you."

Abram and Sarai tried very hard to believe God's promise. It was so hard, though, because they didn't have any children.

"How can God's promise come true when we don't have a baby?" wondered Abram.

"Sometimes it's so hard to believe and trust God," said Sarai.

PROPER 5 [10]

Matthew's Surprise

BASED ON MATTHEW 9:10–13, MARK 2:13–17, LUKE 5:27–32

Matthew was a tax collector. He helped the Romans get money from the Jews.

The Romans came from far away with many soldiers. They said to the Jews, "You have to do what we say. And you have to pay us money. If you don't, our soldiers will kill you."

The Romans used Jewish people like Matthew to help them get the money. That's why most of the Jewish people hated Matthew.

Matthew had done bad things. He had taken money that didn't belong to him. He told lies.

But Matthew was sorry for the bad things he had done. He wanted to help Jesus. He wanted to grow in God's way.

One day, Matthew asked, "Jesus, would you come and have dinner at my house?"

Matthew was surprised when Jesus smiled at him. "I'd like that," Jesus said.

So Matthew asked his other friends to come for dinner, too. Many of them were tax collectors like Matthew. He wanted his friends to meet Jesus.

Some important people heard about Matthew's dinner party. "Why does Jesus do this?" they asked. "Why does Jesus make friends with such bad people? He shouldn't talk to people who cheat and tell lies."

Jesus heard what they were saying. "I'm like a doctor," he said. "Only sick people need a doctor. I've come to help people grow in God's way."

"Well!" said the important people. "We don't need any help from you!"

"Matthew and his friends know they need help," said Jesus sadly. "You important people don't know it. But you need help, too. A lot of help!"

PROPER 5 [10]

Jesus Helps a Sick Girl

BASED ON MATTHEW 9:18–19, 23–26;
MARK 5:21–24, 35–43; LUKE 8:40–42, 49–55

"Please come quick. Please, Jesus," the man cried. "My daughter is very sick. Please come and help her. Please!"

The man's name was Jairus. Jairus was a very important man. He was rich, too.

Right now Jairus didn't feel important. Or rich. He felt afraid. "My little girl is dying," he said to Jesus. "Please come to my house to help her."

So Jesus and Jairus hurried toward the house. Before they got there, someone came running. "Don't bother, Jesus. The girl is dead."

Jairus began to cry. Jesus put his arm around Jairus' shoulders. "Don't be afraid, Jairus," said Jesus. Believe in God's love. And keep walking."

Everyone at the house was in tears.

"Don't cry," said Jesus. "The child isn't dead. She's just sleeping."

Then Jesus took some of his friends and the little girl's mother and father. They went inside. Jesus looked at the little girl. She didn't move. Her face was pale.

"My child," said Jesus. Jesus took the little girl's hand. "Get up."

The girl opened her eyes. She looked at Jesus. She looked at her mom and dad. She smiled just a little.

"How old are you?" Jesus asked.

"Twelve," she said.

"Twelve!" said Jesus. "When I was twelve I was always hungry. Are you hungry?"

The girl nodded.

"Good!" said Jesus. "Why don't we see if we can find you something to eat?"

A Mother of Nations

BASED ON GENESIS 17 – 18:19, 21:1–7

God repeated the promise to Abram and Sarai many times. Each time it was the same promise. Their children's children's children's children would be a great nation.

Each year it got harder and harder to believe the promise, because each year Sarai and Abram got older and older, and they *still* didn't have a baby.

One day, God said to Abram, "Remember my promise. Always remember. And because of my promise, I want you to change your name.

"Right now your name is Abram, which means 'important father.' But from now on your name will be Abraham, which means 'the father of many.'

"And Sarai should change her name, too. Call her Sarah, which means 'princess.' Sarah will be the mother of many nations."

Abraham told Sarah about his talk with God. "But how can that be," he said. "I'm too old to be anybody's father."

Then, one day, when Sarah was working inside the tent and Abraham was sitting under a tree outside, they had some visitors. Sarah looked out through the door of the tent. "Are they sent by God?" she wondered.

Abraham and Sarah were always kind to visitors when they came. So Sarah baked some bread and Abraham got some meat, and soon they had a nice meal ready.

After the meal, while Abraham and the three visitors sat under the tree outside the tent, one of the visitors said something hard to believe.

"I'll be coming back this way in about a year," he said. "By then, Sarah will have had a baby."

Sarah was listening inside the tent. At first she just giggled a little at the idea of it. A woman, as old as a grandmother, having a baby. Then she started to laugh. She laughed so hard she could hardly stop.

"Why is Sarah laughing?" said the man. "Is anything too hard for God?"

"Oh, I didn't laugh," said Sarah.

"You laughed all right," said the man. "But remember, a year from now, you'll have a baby."

When they heard this, Sarah and Abraham both laughed until their sides ached.

Then, one day, it happened. Sarah became pregnant. Even though she was very old, she had a baby.

She and Abraham were so happy as they looked at their tiny baby boy, with his little fists and his tightly closed eyes.

So they gave their baby a special name. They called him Isaac, which means "laughter."

God's promise was coming true after all. Sarah and Abraham knew this as they smiled at the little baby in their arms.

They would become great, great, great, great-grandparents. And all because of God's promise and a baby named Isaac. A baby named Laughter.

Telling the Stories of Jesus

BASED ON MATTHEW 9:35 – 10:8

Note to leaders: *In this story, Jesus sits the disciples down to do some teaching. That teaching is the reading for next Sunday, Proper 7 [12], on page 141.*

Jesus went to many different places to tell people about God's love. Many people came to hear what he had to say.

A group of Jesus' friends went with him to all these places. They were called disciples. One day, Jesus said to them, "I need your help."

"Sure," said Peter. "What would you like us to do?"

"The people who come to listen to me – they seem like children without parents. They seem like sheep without a shepherd."

"I know," said Susanna. "Whenever I see them, I feel sad."

"There are so many places where people want to hear about God's love. But I can't go to all of them. Do you think you might be able to go to some of the places instead of me?"

"We will do our best," said Peter. "Just tell us where to go and what to say."

"You know what to say," said Jesus. "You've heard me talking to all the people. I've talked to them about being kind to each other. I've talked to them about taking care of people who are poor or who are sick. Talk to them about the same things."

"You sometimes help sick people feel better," said Susanna. "I don't know how to do that."

"Sure you do," said Jesus. "Show them how much God loves them. Show them that you love them, too. When people know they are loved, it helps them feel stronger inside."

"Should we go to different countries?" asked Peter. "Or should we stay here in Israel?"

"Stay here in Israel," said Jesus. "When we've told all the people of Israel about God's love, then we can go to other countries.

"When you go to each town, find a kind person to stay with. If the people in that town listen to your stories, then stay there for a while and tell them more about God's love. But if they don't want to hear you talking about God, it's okay. Don't feel sad. Just go on to the next town.

"Listen," said Jesus. "I don't want you to take a lot of clothes or a lot of money or anything else. If people like what you tell them, they'll give you food and a place to sleep."

"I'm a little bit afraid," said Peter. "I've never been to most of those towns and I don't know anyone there."

"Of course you're afraid." Jesus put his hand on Peter's shoulder. "So try hard to remember that God is with you everywhere. All the time! In the daytime and at nighttime. If you can remember that, you will feel strong enough to talk to strangers.

"Now – sit down on the grass under this nice, shady tree. I want to tell you more about how to live God's way."

Hagar Hears God's Promise

BASED ON GENESIS 16:1–16, 21:8–21

Hagar wanted something of her very own.

She had never had anything that belonged to her. Not even her clothes. Not even her own self.

Hagar was a slave. A slave is someone who is owned by somebody else, the way you might own a dog or a cat. Hagar's owner was Sarah. Sarah was married to Abraham.

Sarah wanted a baby. God had promised her a baby, but she was getting old and she started to worry that maybe there would never be a baby. So Sarah had a plan. In those days, if a woman could not have a baby, she could ask another woman to help her.

"Abraham," Sarah said one day, "I want you to have sex with my slave, Hagar, so that she will have our baby. Because Hagar is my slave, the baby will belong to me and it will be as if the baby really came out of my body."

So that's what happened. Sarah and Abraham didn't ask Hagar if it was okay. They just went and did it.

When Hagar got pregnant she felt important. People said nice things and talked about her baby. But sometimes she teased Sarah. "I can have a baby and you can't." Then Sarah got so angry that Hagar had to run away.

But God talked with Hagar when she was hiding from Sarah. "Hagar, right now you have to think of your baby. Go back and live with Sarah and do what she tells you. But remember this, Hagar. You will give birth to a child of the promise. A good name for the child would be Ishmael, which means, 'God hears.' God hears you, Hagar, and God will hear Ishmael, and from you will come a great nation of many people."

Then Hagar said to God, "I don't know your name, but I will call you, The God of Seeing. That will be your name from me, and for Ishmael and for all the people of the promise." So Hagar went back to live with Sarah, even though it was a hard thing to do.

When the baby came out of Hagar's body, she knew it was her baby, but Sarah told her friends, "See! I have a baby now." Then Hagar felt as if everything had been taken away from her again.

One day, Sarah had a baby of her own. She named him Isaac. God talked to Sarah and Abraham about their baby, too, and told them Isaac would also be the father of a great nation of people. That made them very, very happy.

It made Hagar very worried, because she knew that meant danger for Ishmael. Hagar began to wonder if God really had made that promise, or whether she had just been dreaming.

One day Ishmael and Isaac were playing together. Sarah saw them and called Abraham, "Get that kid and his mother out of here. I don't want him playing with my Isaac. God has promised to make Isaac's descendants into a great nation, so we don't need Ishmael anymore. The promise is just for us!"

"But Sarah," said Abraham. "You wanted Ishmael for your own son before Isaac came. I can't just kick them out. Where would they go?"

"Just get rid of them!" shouted Sarah.

So Abraham gave Hagar a leather bag of water and some food and told her to go with Ishmael into the desert. Hagar could hardly believe that Abraham and Sarah would do such a thing. There was no food or people or anything out in the desert.

Soon the food and water were gone. Hagar tried so hard to keep going, but Ishmael got weaker and weaker. He couldn't walk anymore.

Hagar put Ishmael under a bush and walked away. She couldn't bear to hear him cry. She didn't want to watch him die.

Hagar felt angry at God. "Why did you let this happen to us?" she yelled. "Why God? Why do we have to die like this?"

"Hagar!" God spoke gently inside her. "Sarah and Abraham don't understand. The promise is not just for one person or one tribe. The promise is for you and for Ishmael, too. Ishmael will get married and you will have grandchildren and many, many great-grandchildren."

Hagar began to cry. Until now, she had been too angry to cry, but when she heard God's voice in her heart, she began to believe the promise again. She remembered how she had talked with God when she ran away from Sarah, how she had given God a name and God had given her a name for Ishmael, and how God had made a promise to her.

And then, through her tears, Hagar saw a well. Water! There in the desert!

Hagar ran and got Ishmael. She put some water on his dry lips and got him to drink. Soon he began to feel strong again. Then Hagar drank, and she felt strong, too. Again, she was able to believe God's promise.

"Ishmael," she said. "All my life I wanted something of my very own. Now I have it. I have God's promise. We both have God's promise, Ishmael, and we have each other. We are not slaves anymore. We are free to be God's children."

Then Hagar stood up tall. She raised her arms up wide to the whole sky.

In a strong, quiet voice, Hagar said, "Thank you, God."

Jesus Teaches His Friends

BASED ON MATTHEW 10:24–39

Jesus asked his friends to go to many places in Israel. He wanted them to tell everyone how much God loves them.

"But I have some other things to say to you," he said. "Sit down on the grass with me. Under this shady tree."

So Jesus' friends all sat down. They listened very hard. Here are some of the things Jesus said to them.

"When you are teaching people about God's love, remember that God loves them as much as God loves you.

"Don't be afraid of the people you meet. Remember that God cares for them just as God cares for you. You can go to the market and buy two tiny birds for money. But God thinks you are more important than many, many birds. God loves you so much that God even knows how many hairs you have on your head.

"When you tell my stories, some people may not want to hear them. Sometimes people will be angry at you. Some of them may even hurt you. Some people don't want to be kind to others. They don't want to help people who are sick or who are poor. It's not easy to live God's way. But those who listen to me and who try to live in God's way will find that they will be strong enough to do it. They will feel God's love."

"I'm still afraid to go out to strange places to tell those stories," said Peter.

"So am I," said Susanna.

"Of course you are afraid. So am I." said Jesus. "When you are afraid, God will be with you. Like a best friend. Like a mother, or a father. You will still be afraid, but you will feel strong enough to do it anyway."

Abraham Doesn't Understand

BASED ON GENESIS 22

This story is scary. It would be best to read it with an adult and then talk about it afterwards.

In Bible times, some people thought God wanted them to hurt other people. Sometimes they thought God wanted them to kill other people in wars. God never wants that.

Sometimes adults think it's okay to hurt children or each other. That isn't true. God never wants people to hurt each other. That's one of the reasons this story is in the Bible.

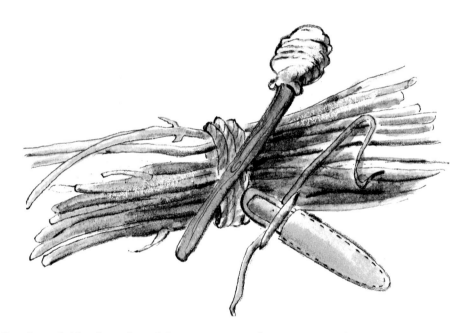

Sarah and Abraham loved Isaac very much. Isaac was the only child they had, born when they were both very old.

Sometimes Abraham and Sarah would say to each other, "We are very rich people. We own lots of sheep and goats and we have many people working for us. But we'd give them all away to keep Isaac."

Sarah and Abraham loved Isaac. They loved God, too. They always tried so hard to do whatever God wanted them to do.

Often, they would have a sacrifice for God. They would take a lamb or a goat. Then they would build a big fire on a pile of rocks they called an altar. They would kill the lamb or goat and burn it on the fire. Abraham and Sarah felt this was a good way to show their love for God.

One day, God called, "Abraham."

"I'm here, God," said Abraham.

"I want you to take your son, Isaac, whom you love so much. Go to a place called Moriah, where I will show you a mountain. There I want you to make a sacrifice, but I want you to use Isaac, not a lamb or a goat."

Abraham could hardly believe God would want him to do such a thing. He cried all night long and asked God over and over again, "Please, not Isaac. You can have anything I own, but please, not Isaac. He's our only child."

In the morning, Abraham knew that he had to do it. So he got some wood, and a sharp knife, and a burning torch to light the fire. Abraham also asked two of his servants to help carry things. And of course, he took Isaac.

They travelled for two days and two nights. On the third day while they were walking, Abraham told the servants to stay behind. "Isaac and I will go up the mountain and make our sacrifice," he said. "Wait here, please."

"Dad," Isaac asked, "we have wood for the sacrifice, and we have a torch to light the fire. How come we don't have a lamb or a goat for the sacrifice?"

Abraham seemed to take a long time to answer Isaac's question. Then he said, "God will give us something for the sacrifice."

Isaac didn't understand, but he didn't mind. He often didn't understand the things his dad said about God.

When they finally got to the right place, Abraham took the wood and piled it on the altar.

Then Abraham took Isaac in his arms and gave him a long, long hug. Very quietly and gently he said, "Isaac, my son, I love you so very, very much. I want you to know that, Isaac."

"I know that, Father," said Isaac. "And I love you, too."

Then Abraham tied Isaac with some ropes. "Why are you doing that?" Isaac asked.

Abraham didn't say anything, but he kissed Isaac very gently, and put him on top of the altar. Isaac could hear his dad say some quiet words, as if Abraham was praying.

Then, all of a sudden, Abraham pulled off the ropes. He picked up Isaac and hugged him. There were tears streaming down Abraham's face, but he was smiling.

"Isaac! Oh, Isaac, my son!" Abraham said. "Look over there. In the bush. There's a sheep God has given us for the sacrifice."

"But, Dad, why did you tie me up on the altar. Were you going to sacrifice me?"

"Yes, Isaac. It was a test. I had to be willing to give up my most precious thing to prove that I loved God. That's what God told me to do."

"But you didn't," said Isaac.

"No," said Abraham. "Just when I was going to do it, an angel said to me, 'Abraham, don't you touch that boy! Now I know that you love God more than anything.' I was so happy to hear that message from God. Now I know I can love you, Isaac, and love God, too.

"I also learned something else. God doesn't want us to hurt each other."

So Abraham and Isaac took the sheep that was caught in the bush, and they made a sacrifice to God. As part of their sacrifice they said, "Thank you, God."

Then, once more, God told Abraham about the promise. "You will have more great, great, great, great-grandchildren than there are stars in the sky.

"They will remember you, Abraham. They will remember that you were willing to give up anything, even your son, Isaac, for God."

Abigail Does Something for God

BASED ON MATTHEW 10:40–42

Thomas was limping. Just a little. "I have a sore foot," he said to Jesus.
"What happened?"

"I was walking along the road," said Thomas. "And I was watching some children playing games. I didn't look where I was going, and I bumped my toe against a big rock. It hurts! I guess I yelled pretty loud, because the children stopped playing. One of them came and asked, 'Are you hurt?'"

"That was a kind thing to do," said Jesus.

"Yes. Then she went into her house and got some water and some bandages. She washed the toe and put the bandages on."

"Did you move the stone that hurt your foot?"

Thomas looked surprised. "I should have thought of that."

"We'll be walking down that road this afternoon," said Jesus. "We can move the stone then and hope nobody else hurts their toe."

That afternoon, Jesus and Thomas found the stone. It was quite big and heavy. They both had to lift to move it off the road.

"See those children over there?" said Thomas. "That girl, the tall one? See, she and that boy are playing. She's the one that came to help me."

Jesus walked over to the girl. "Thank you for helping my sore toe. That was very kind."

The girl looked surprised. "I didn't help your toe."

Jesus smiled. "I know. But in a way you did. You helped one of my friends, and so you helped me."

The girl looked puzzled for a moment. Then she laughed. "I guess so!" she said.

"What's your name?" asked Jesus.

"Abigail."

"Enjoy your game, Abigail," said Jesus. Abigail smiled and ran off to play ball with her friend.

"Why did you say that?" asked Thomas.

"Because it's true. You are my friend. I care about you. So in a way, you are a part of me. So if someone is nice to you, they are nice to me."

"That means," said Thomas, "that if someone is nice to you, Jesus, they are also being nice to me."

"Yes. But here is something even better. When that girl was kind to you, she was being kind to God. God loves you. So if someone does something nice for you, they're doing it to God."

"Does that mean if I do something bad to that girl, I'm doing something bad to God?"

"Yes. Because God loves that girl and she is part of God."

"Then God loves everybody!"

"That's right, Thomas. Suppose you see an old man lying beside the road. His clothes are all torn, and he has no place to live. He looks as if he needs a bath. He has no friends. If you give that poor old man even just a glass of cold water on a hot day, it's as if you are giving that drink to God."

Rebekah and Isaac

BASED ON GENESIS 24

Sarah was 127 years old when she died. Isaac was a grown man by this time. He cried when his mother died. Isaac and his father, Abraham, buried her in a special place, which they bought from some of the people who lived nearby.

Before Sarah died, she and Isaac and Abraham had some long talks about God's promise. Now Isaac remembered those talks with his mother and he felt very lonely.

"Isaac," said Abraham. "You need to get married."

"But, Dad…" Isaac started to say.

"Never mind. Do what I say. You can't marry any of the women around here," Abraham said. "They don't live in God's way. They don't understand about God's promise."

"But, Dad…" Isaac tried again.

"Just be quiet and listen," said Abraham. "I'll send one of my servants to the place where we used to live, long before you were born, Isaac. We have lots of uncles and aunts and cousins living there. They don't know about God's promise, but they try to live in God's way. Maybe the servant can find the right person for you to marry."

So Abraham sent one of his servants, a man named Eliezer, to a town called Nahor, where Abraham's relatives still lived. He made Eliezer promise to find just the right woman.

To help the servant, Abraham sent along ten camels loaded down with good things. These were gifts Eliezer could give to Abraham's relatives.

When Eliezer got to Nahor, he was hot and tired. He stopped to rest in the shade of some trees that grew near a well. While he was resting, Eliezer watched the people come to the well to get water.

The servant prayed to God, "Please help me choose the right person." Just then he saw Rebekah coming to the well.

"Could you give me a drink of water?" he said to Rebekah.

"Of course," she said. And then without being asked, she gave water to all ten camels, too.

That was hard work, because camels drink lots and lots of water. The well was very deep. She was quite tired by the time she finished. But she didn't mind. Rebekah felt it was important to be kind to strangers. She often offered to help people when they seemed to need it.

The servant smiled as he watched Rebekah carry water to his camels. "I think this is the woman God would like me to bring to Isaac, so they can share the promise together."

"Thank you," said Abraham's servant, when Rebekah had finished. "Is there room at your house for me to spend the night?"

"Of course," said Rebekah. "We've got lots of room and food for you and for your camels."

There was lots to talk about at Rebekah's house that night. They invited

Eliezer to have supper with them. Before he would eat, he had to tell them all the news about Abraham and Sarah and Isaac. And, of course, he explained why he had come.

"I think God wants me to invite Rebekah to share the promise with Isaac," Eliezer said.

Rebekah's mother, and her brother, and all the rest of the family didn't know what to think. They talked about whether Rebekah should or shouldn't go. Nobody said, "Let's go ask Rebekah."

Finally they all agreed. Rebekah should go. That's when Eliezer brought out all the wonderful gifts he had brought. He gave them all to Rebekah's family.

They all talked as if it didn't matter what Rebekah thought. The next day someone said, "Maybe we should ask Rebekah."

So they did.

"I'll go," said Rebekah. "Right now."

"Right now?" said her mother. "Couldn't you wait for a week or so?"

"No, I want to go right now," Rebekah insisted.

The servant smiled to himself. "She can think for herself," he thought. "She's not only got a strong body, she's got a strong spirit, too. Rebekah and Isaac will like each other."

The next morning they all left. The servant and his helpers and all ten camels, and Rebekah and all her helpers. There were lots of hugs and tears and goodbyes, and then they set off.

It took many days to get to where Isaac lived in Canaan. Rebekah didn't like riding on camels one bit. Sometimes she felt sick because the camels would sway back and forth. Once she had to throw up. Sometimes she hated the smell of the camels. Sometimes she was just plain bored. It was a long trip.

One day, Eliezer told her, "We're getting close to Canaan now." Rebekah began to get excited. When she saw a man walking in a field she asked Eliezer, "Who's that?"

"That," said Eliezer, "is Isaac. He's the man you have come to marry."

"Make the camel kneel so I can get off," said Rebekah. Then she began walking across the field toward Isaac.

Isaac saw Rebekah coming across the field. They had never seen each other before, and yet they knew they were going to be husband and wife.

Both Rebekah and Isaac had thought of things they would say to each other when they met. Now neither could think of anything. They walked together toward the tent where Sarah, Isaacs's mother, had lived.

Rebekah and Isaac were married in that tent.

In time, they came to love each other very deeply. And Rebekah often thanked God because of the promise that she and Isaac shared.

Children Know This

BASED ON MATTHEW 11:16–19, 25–27

Jesus and his friends spent the whole day in the marketplace. Jesus was telling stories to anyone who would listen. His friends helped people understand the stories.

Some of the people didn't want to listen. "Jesus is trying to tell us that God is everywhere and loves everybody. That's not true. God only likes the good people like us."

In the evening, Jesus was very tired. Some of his friends brought some food to him. "Let's sit down and have something to eat and drink," they said. They gave Jesus some bread and some cheese and some figs. And they gave him something to drink.

Some of the people who didn't like Jesus saw this. "Look," they said. "Jesus eats and drinks just like everybody else. How can he be God's prophet if he eats and drinks just like us?"

Jesus didn't answer them. He was just too tired. But after they had eaten and rested for a while, Jesus began to feel better.

"Those people!" said Jesus, shaking his head slowly. "What do they want? When John the Baptizer came, he hardly ate or drank anything. And he wasn't friends with anybody. So they all said, 'He's weird! How can he be God's prophet if he doesn't eat and drink like everybody else?' Now I'm here, and I get hungry and thirsty like everybody else. So I eat and I drink like everybody else. I have lots of friends. And those people say, 'How can he be God's prophet if he eats and drinks like all the rest of us? How can he be a good person if he is friends with people who aren't good?'"

"Try not to worry about it, Jesus," said Susanna. "You can't make them happy. They don't like anybody who talks about God."

"It reminds me of a little poem," said Jesus.

> I played my flute, so nice and sweet,
> but you wouldn't dance.
> I cried out loud, all through the street,
> but you were in a trance.

"What's a trance?" said Susanna.

"It's like having a dream, except you're not asleep. So many people are walking around as if they are asleep. They don't notice the things that are happening."

"Children notice," said Susanna. "Do you remember Abigail, the girl who helped Thomas when he hurt his toe?"

Jesus nodded.

"Well, I saw her helping someone else today," said Susanna.

"She knows we should be kind to other people," said Jesus. "All other people! And she's a child."

Susanna shook her head slowly. "How come so many children know this? But so many adults don't?"

Rebekah and Her Babies

BASED ON GENESIS 25

After Rebekah and Isaac were married, they began hoping for a baby. It didn't happen.

Sometimes Rebekah would say to Isaac, "I'm beginning to know what your mom felt like. She was 90 years old before you came along. Will I have to wait that long?"

Rebekah didn't wait quite that long. Twenty years after they were married, she said to her husband, "Isaac, we're pregnant."

She didn't have an easy time. Rebekah knew she would feel the baby moving inside her, but it seemed this baby was jumping around far too much.

So Rebekah asked God about it. God gave her a bigger answer than she expected.

"You are having twins, Rebekah," said God. "Each of the twins will grow up to be the grandparent of many people, the great-great-grandparent of a whole nation. It's part of the promise I made to Abraham and Sarah."

When the twins were born, they turned out to be two boys. The first baby to be born seemed all red and hairy. They named him Esau, which means "hairy."

The second twin came out of Rebekah right after the first. He came so close, he seemed to be hanging onto the heel of his brother. So they named him Jacob, which means "he grabs what doesn't belong to him."

As the boys grew older, Esau liked to go out hunting for food in the hills. That made Isaac, his father, happy. Jacob liked to stay around home with his mother, so Rebekah liked him the best.

Esau and Jacob often got angry at each other. "I'm the oldest," said Esau. "Father will give me everything when he dies. You won't get anything."

It was true. Esau was older by about one minute. In those days, the oldest son got almost everything when his father died. Younger sons got just a little. Girls didn't get anything.

"It's not fair," Rebekah often said to Jacob. "You should have your father's sheep and cows and goats. We've got to figure out a way to make it happen."

One day, Jacob was cooking up a tasty stew for himself and Rebekah. It smelled wonderful. Jacob was a good cook.

Just then Esau came in from hunting. He hadn't caught anything, so he hadn't eaten for two days. He was very, very hungry. "Give me some of your stew!" he said to Jacob.

Now Jacob saw his chance. "I'll give you some of my stew if you promise to let me have all the things Dad plans to give to you."

"Who cares?" Esau yelled. "You can have anything you want. If I don't eat right away, I'll die anyway."

"Promise?" asked Jacob.

"Yes, promise! Now give me some food!"

Jacob smiled. He knew he would get something that didn't belong to him. He ran to tell his mother about it.

Esau didn't think about what he had just done. He was too busy eating.

Stories That Help Us Grow

BASED ON MATTHEW 13:3–12, 18–23;
MARK 4:3–9, 13–20; LUKE 8:5–15

Jesus liked stories. He remembered the stories Mary and Joseph told him when he was a child. Jesus made up stories, too. Sometimes he made up stories just for fun. Sometimes he made up parables so people would understand about God's love. Those stories helped people grow in God's way.

People liked those parables. "We can understand Jesus because he explains things with stories," they said.

Here is one of the parables Jesus told.

The farmer went out to sow some seeds. He wanted to grow some grain to make bread. "I'm going to plant lots of seeds everywhere," said the farmer.

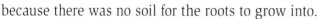

The farmer put a bunch of seeds where people walked. But the ground was too hard. Then birds came and ate the seeds.

"Well, that didn't work," said the farmer.

So the farmer put a bunch of seeds in rocky places. There was hardly any soil. At first the seeds grew very fast. Then they died, because there was no soil for the roots to grow into.

"Well, that didn't work," said the farmer.

So the farmer put seeds among the weeds. The seeds started to grow. But the weeds grew faster and killed the grain seeds.

"Well, that didn't work," said the farmer.

Then the farmer put seeds on good soil. The soil was nice and soft. There was lots of water. Soon the seeds grew into good strong plants.

"Well, that really worked," said the farmer. "Now I'll have lots of grain to eat."

When Jesus told the story, his friends looked very puzzled.

"We don't know what the story means," they said. So Jesus told them.

"God is like that farmer," said Jesus. "God plants lots of love in our hearts. But somebody has hurt us and the love doesn't grow.

"Or sometimes we are very happy when we feel God's love. We sing and dance. But later, we forget about it.

"Or sometimes we're too busy. Or we think about too many other things. We don't have time for God's love.

"Sometimes we let God's love really grow inside us. When that happens, we love other people. Then they know about God's love, too."

Jacob Steals from Esau

BASED ON GENESIS 27

Note to leaders: This story (based on Genesis 27) is not included the lectionary, but is a good one to share with children – and adults! – because it fills in the details they need in order to understand the lectionary story for this week, which immediately follows the story below.

"I don't think Esau even remembers what he promised you," Rebekah said one day.

"But a promise is a promise," said Jacob.

"Maybe," said Rebekah, "but your father, Isaac, doesn't know about it. And one day he will give Esau his blessing. That means everything he has, all his goats and his sheep and everything, will belong to Esau. Esau will get everything, even though Esau said you would have it."

"So what can we do?"

"I'm not sure," said Rebekah. "But I'm always near your father. He's so old and blind now. I have to take care of him all the time. I'll look for a chance."

One day, it happened. "Tell Esau I want to talk to him," old Isaac said to Rebekah. So Rebekah went and called Esau. Then she stood outside of their tent and listened to what Isaac said.

"Esau, my son." Isaac took Esau's hairy hands into his. "I am getting very old. I can't see anymore, and I can't walk. I think I am going to die soon. Before I die, I want to give you my blessing."

"Oh no, Father," said Esau. "You're not going to die. You'll be able to see again."

"It's all right," said Isaac. "I have had a good life and I am ready to die. Now go out and hunt something to eat. Bring it back here and make a tasty dinner for me. When I've eaten the food, I'll give you my blessing."

"Yes, Father." Esau ran off to get his bow and arrows. Rebekah ran off to find Jacob.

"Listen, Jacob." Rebekah talked very fast. "Go get a goat quickly. Kill it so I can cook it just the way your dad likes it. And here. Tie this goat skin on your neck and on your hands so you feel as hairy as Esau. Get some of Esau's clothes so you smell like him, too."

Jacob took the food in and tried to trick his dad. "I'm back, Dad," he said, trying to make his voice sound like Esau's. "God helped me catch something very fast, so I cooked it just the way you like it."

Old Isaac reached out to touch Jacob as he gave him the food. "Your voice sounds like Jacob," Isaac said. "But your hands feel like Esau's."

Then the old man ate the food. He still wasn't quite sure it was Esau, so he said, "Come close to me so I can kiss you." When Jacob came close, Isaac could smell Esau's clothes, the clothes of a hunter. Then he thought it really was Esau.

So Isaac blessed Jacob. "May God give you every good thing," he said. "May

the promise that God made to your grandparents, Sarah and Abraham, be your promise, too. And everything that I own is yours, my son."

Soon after Isaac got up and left, Esau came in. "Here is the food I have cooked for you," he said.

"Who are you?" Isaac asked.

"I am Esau, your oldest son. I have come for your blessing."

Isaac started to shake all over. "Who was it that just brought me some food? Because whoever it was, I have given him my blessing."

"It's that Jacob again," yelled Esau. "He keeps taking what doesn't belong to him! He cheats me out of everything!"

"Yes," said Isaac. "Your brother came and lied to me, and he took your blessing."

"Can't you give me a blessing, too?" Esau asked. He was crying now. "Please, Dad, can't you bless me, too?"

"No, Esau, I can't. I'm so sorry, but I can't. What I have done, I have done. I can't change it."

Esau was very, very angry. "I'm going to kill Jacob for what he did," he thought to himself. "I'm going to kill him."

Rebekah knew how angry Esau was. So she said to Jacob, "You have to run away. Go right now."

"But where can I go, Mother?" asked Jacob.

"Go to my brother, Laban, who lives in Haran. Go stay with him until Esau stops being angry. Then you can come back home."

So Jacob ran away to Haran.

Jacob had cheated his brother. Now his father was very sad. His brother was angry. His mother had told him to run away. He wouldn't get his father's sheep and goats after all.

Jacob wasn't very happy. And Rebekah cried because Jacob wasn't home anymore.

Jacob's Dream

BASED ON GENESIS 28:10–22

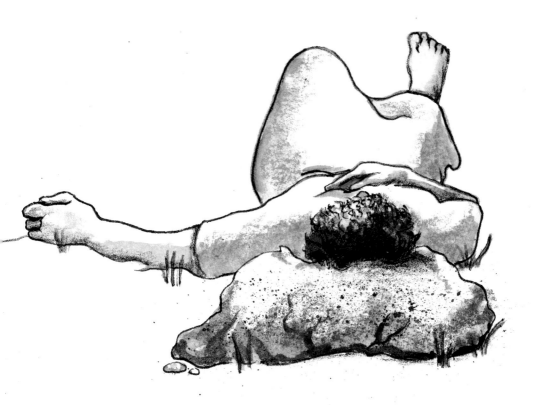

Jacob was running away. He had cheated his brother and lied to his father. He was afraid.

Jacob's mother, Rebekah, had told him to run to Haran, to the place where her brother, Laban, lived. But Jacob didn't even know where Haran was.

Jacob ran and ran until he was so tired, he could hardly stand up. It was getting dark and he was afraid. Over and over he thought about what he had done.

Jacob knew that Isaac's blessing meant God's promise of a great nation was now his. God had made the promise to Abraham and Sarah, then it had been passed on to Rebekah and Isaac.

Now it was his. But as Jacob stood there alone in the dark, feeling cold and hungry, God's promise didn't seem to help very much.

Finally, Jacob was so tired he lay down on the hard ground. He put his head on a rock. "Some pillow," he thought to himself. In the middle of the night, some-

thing happened.
Maybe it was just a
dream.

Jacob didn't think it was a
dream, because it was all so real.
Jacob was sure he saw a bright light from
up in the sky. Then there were stairs that began
right beside him on the ground and reached all the
way up into the sky.

"There were angels on the stairs," Jacob told his children
many years later. "Angels going up the stairs, and angels coming
down. And at the very top, there was God."

"Then God spoke to me," said Jacob. "God said, 'I am
the God of your grandparents, Abraham and Sarah, and of
your parents, Isaac and Rebekah. The promise is now yours,
Jacob. You will be the great-great-grandfather of many, many
people. People all over the world will learn about me, because of you. And Jacob, I will be with you. I am your
God. I will take care of you.'"

The next morning Jacob woke up. Well, he wasn't sure if
he woke up because he wasn't sure if he had been sleeping.
But he did remember what he had seen. Or dreamed.

So Jacob took the stone he had used for a
pillow, and he set it up on end. "This place is special,
because I've seen God here," Jacob said to himself.

"I'm going to call this place Bethel, which means,
'the house of God.' And from now on, I will give
one-tenth of everything I own to God."

The next morning, as Jacob walked along, he thought and thought about God's promise, and about what kind of person God wanted him to be.

Jacob still didn't know where Haran was. He was still alone and hungry. All he had were the clothes on his back and his walking stick.

But somehow, Jacob felt much better after his strange experience the night before.

The Wheat and the Weeds

BASED ON MATTHEW 13:24–30, 36–43

"God has a dream for us," Jesus told his friends. "God wants us to live in a way that would make everyone happy. I like to call that 'God's shalom.'"

"I don't understand that word…sha…whatever," said James.

"Sha-LOM." Jesus said it slowly so James would know how to say it. "Shalom rhymes with home. It's a wonderful word that has a big meaning. Here is a story that will help you understand part of it."

Jesus' friends liked his parables. So they all sat down to listen.

"God's shalom is like this. There was a farmer who had a big field. He planted wheat seeds over the whole field. And the wheat began to grow. It looked like a nice green lawn.

"But in the middle of the night, the wind blew different seeds on the field. Weeds. Plants that didn't belong there. So when the wheat grew tall, so did the weeds.

"One of the people who helped the farmer came and asked, 'What shall we do? Do you want me to go onto the field and pull out all the weeds?'

"'No, don't do that!' said the farmer. 'If you pull out the weeds, you will pull out the wheat, too. Just let the weeds and the wheat grow together.'

"So that's what they did. When the wheat was big and tall, it turned into a nice golden color. 'Now it's time to gather the seeds of the wheat,' said the farmer. 'But take the weeds and put them all in one pile. Then I will burn the weeds. But I will keep the wheat.'"

"I still don't get it," said James.

Jesus smiled. "I told you 'shalom' is a big word. And I will tell you more stories to help you understand.

"But let me help you understand this parable about the wheat, Thomas. You can see many good things happening, can't you?"

"Oh yes. Remember Abigail, who helped me when I hurt my toe. And I know a man who goes out every morning to feed people who are hungry. And..."

"Many people are doing good things, all over the world," said Jesus. "That's the wheat in the story."

"So the weeds in the story are the bad things that happen?"

"Yes. You see, you do understand, Thomas. Some people are doing bad things."

"I saw two people fighting yesterday," said Thomas. "They were hurting each other. And there are people in our town who don't have enough to eat. And..."

"The bad things happening are like the weeds. The good things happening are like the wheat. In God's shalom, we'll all work together, just like the farmer and the helper, to gather the golden wheat and burn up the weeds."

Jacob Falls in Love

BASED ON GENESIS 29

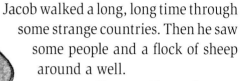

Jacob walked a long, long time through some strange countries. Then he saw some people and a flock of sheep around a well.

"Hello!" said Jacob. "Do you know the way to Haran?"

"Yes," said the shepherds, "we live in Haran."

"Oh," said Jacob. "Then do you know a man named Laban?"

"Sure we do."

"Can you tell me the way to his house?" asked Jacob. "Laban is my uncle."

"We can do even better than that." One of the shepherds pointed to some sheep coming toward the well. "The person leading those sheep is Rachel, one of Laban's daughters."

Jacob didn't know what to say or do. But he could see that Rachel had come to the well to give her sheep a drink. Jacob ran over to the well, and moved the stone that covered it. It was a huge stone.

"Look at that man move that stone," said one of the other shepherds. "How come he's strong enough to move it all by himself?"

"He must be in love," said another shepherd.

Jacob gave a drink to all of Rachel's sheep. Then he gave her a kiss. Then he started to cry.

Rachel didn't know what to think. She ran home and told her father.

In those days, a woman and a man couldn't just decide to marry each other. They had to ask the woman's father. Fathers believed their daughters belonged to them. Sometimes, fathers would sell their daughters the way they might sell a sheep or a goat.

Jacob didn't have anything except his clothes and his walking stick. He knew he had nothing to give Rachel's father. So Jacob went to Rachel's father and asked for a job.

Jacob began to work for Laban, taking care of the sheep and goats. He worked very hard.

After Jacob had been working for Laban for a whole month, he said, "I want to marry Rachel. I love her very much. If I work for you for seven years, can I marry her?"

"Sure," said Laban.

Jacob didn't know that Laban was not very honest. In fact, Laban liked to trick people. Like Jacob, Laban tried to grab things that didn't belong to him.

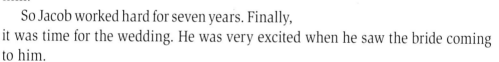

So Jacob worked hard for seven years. Finally, it was time for the wedding. He was very excited when he saw the bride coming to him.

Jacob wanted to see her eyes. "I wonder if she is as happy and as excited as I am?" he thought. But her face was covered with a dark veil. That's what brides always wore in those days.

The wedding party lasted far into the night. The next morning when Jacob woke up, he found himself in bed with Leah, Rachel's older sister.

Jacob was very angry. Leah was a nice person, but Jacob was in love with Rachel.

"Why have you done this to me?" Jacob yelled at Laban. "I worked seven years so I could marry Rachel. Now you made Leah marry me. Why?"

"In our country, the younger daughter can't get married until the older daughter is married," said Laban. "Rachel can't get married until Leah is married."

"So what should I do?" asked Jacob.

"It's simple," Laban laughed. "You can marry more than one woman. Go ahead. You can marry Rachel now, too. Then you can work for seven more years to pay for her."

"Well, all right," Jacob shrugged.

Then Jacobs's eyes got very big. He knew what had happened. He had been tricked. Just as Jacob had tricked his brother, now Jacob had been tricked.

Neither Laban nor Jacob even wondered how Leah and Rachel felt about all this.

Stories of God's Shalom

BASED ON MATTHEW 13:31–33, 44–45

Shalom is a Hebrew word. It means something like "peace," but it means more than that. Jesus told many parables to help us understand shalom. Maybe he was laughing a little when he told this one.

"God's shalom is like a mustard seed," Jesus said as he held the tiny seed in his hand. "See how tiny it is?"

"You think a mustard seed can only grow into a small plant? Well, pretend that it can grow big as a tree. Pretend that birds will come and make nests in its branches."

Everyone laughed. "A mustard plant as big as a tree?"

"Yes," Jesus laughed, too. "God's shalom is like that."

Then Jesus told an even funnier story.

"You know the yeast people use to make bread? You can't see how the yeast works. It just bubbles around inside the bread.

"Well, suppose a woman took a tiny bit of yeast. Suppose she mixed it with a lot of flour and water. The yeast would work inside the dough. After a while, she would have enough bread to feed a hundred people!"

"You mean one tiny bit of yeast could make all that flour into bread?" someone asked.

"That's right," Jesus smiled. "God's shalom is like that. You can't see it working. But it's there all the time, working in you and working in me."

"Here is another way to think about God's shalom," said Jesus.

"God's shalom is like a treasure hidden in a field. If you knew about that treasure, you would go and sell all the things you had. Then you would take the money and buy the whole field. You would want the treasure to be yours."

"Should we want God's shalom that much?" the people asked.

"Yes," said Jesus. "That much!"

Jacob Fights with God

BASED ON GENESIS 31, 32, 33

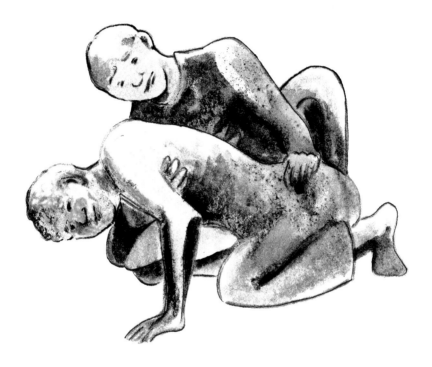

Jacob and Rachel and Leah stayed with Laban a long time. Leah had lots of children. There was a girl named Dinah and 11 boys. Rachel had one baby and his name was Joseph.

All of them worked hard. They took good care of the goats and sheep and donkeys. The family became quite rich.

One day, God told Jacob it was time to go back to his home. Jacob was afraid when God said this. Jacob remembered the tricks he had played on his brother, Esau.

"Maybe," he thought, "if I give lots of presents to my brother, maybe he won't be angry anymore."

So Rachel and Leah and Jacob and all their children and all the people who helped them, and all the sheep and goats and donkeys began to move back to Canaan. There were so many, it looked like a whole town moving all at once.

Jacob was still very worried. Sometimes he was afraid that Esau would kill him. Sometimes Jacob was really sorry for what he had done.

One night, Jacob had asked all the others to go ahead a little ways. "I just want to be by myself tonight," he said.

He never forgot that night. Jacob wasn't sure if it was a dream or not, but if it was a dream, it was a real nightmare.

Jacob seemed to be fighting with someone. Or something. When he tried move, it felt as if someone was holding him. Sometimes Jacob felt as if he was fighting with himself. Sometimes it felt as if he was fighting with the wrong things he had done. Sometimes Jacob felt as if he was fighting with God.

Jacob fought all night. Just before morning, he screamed in pain. Whoever, or whatever he was fighting with, touched the top of his leg and hurt him badly.

Then it seemed as if the fighting was over, and Jacob could talk with whoever it was.

"What is your name?" this strange person seemed to ask.

"My name is Jacob."

"Now your name will be changed. Your name won't be Jacob anymore. Your name will be Israel, which means, 'you struggled with God and with other people.'"

And that is why the Hebrews began to call themselves "the people of Israel."

Just then, the sun began to rise. Jacob wasn't sure if it had been a dream or not. Then he realized it couldn't all have been a dream, because his leg was very sore and it was hard to walk.

Very soon after that, Jacob sent many sheep and goats and donkeys ahead to Esau, hoping Esau wouldn't be angry anymore.

When Jacob saw Esau coming, he saw a smile on Esau's face. Esau threw his arms around his brother, and gave him a big hug and a kiss. And then they both had a good cry. They knew they could be brothers again. Jacob knew that God had forgiven him because Esau forgave him.

Often at night, Jacob would lie awake thinking about all the things that had happened. Jacob would think about that night when he had a fight with the angel. Or was it an angel? Jacob was never sure.

But Jacob knew that part of the fighting had been with the part in himself that was running away from God. He had told many lies and cheated many people. Jacob knew that was wrong.

Jacob wondered how God's promise could still be with him, when he didn't seem to be living in God's way. Then he thought about his new name, Israel. Somehow, Jacob knew that the name was not just for him alone, but for his whole family. It was for Leah and Rachel, for all their children and for all the people who helped them.

They would be called "the people of Israel," the people who had struggled with God – the people who had struggled to know God's promise.

Rachel Dies Having a Baby

BASED ON GENESIS 35

Note to leaders: This story is not included in the lectionary, but is included here to help children understand the stories that follow.

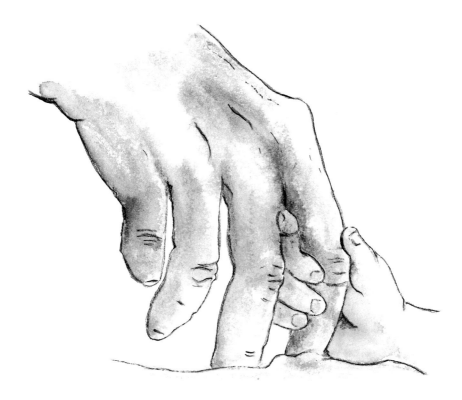

There were quite a lot of people in the house of Israel. By this time, some of the children had grown up and there were grandchildren.

Everyone lived in tents and moved from place to place. They were always looking for nice green grass, for the sheep and goats and donkeys to eat.

Rachel and Leah liked to talk to each other. Rachel sometimes asked, "How come you have such an easy time having babies, Leah? It's always so hard for me."

Of course, Leah didn't know the answer. She always tried to help her sister. Rachel had one baby while they were still living with Laban, their father. The baby's name was Joseph.

Rachel wanted to have more babies. One day she gave Leah a big hug. "Leah. Guess what? I'm pregnant!" The two sisters did a little dance, they were so happy.

But when the baby came, they were not happy. Rachel had a very hard time when this baby was being born. Leah and the other women who were helping did everything they could, but Rachel died.

Leah and Jacob were very sad when this happened. Both of them had loved Rachel very much. They buried Rachel in the ground and put up a big stone to mark the place.

This happened near the town of Bethlehem. For many years, people remembered Rachel when they saw the stone over her grave.

Though Rachel died, the baby was fine. It was a boy, and they named him Benjamin.

There was other sadness in the house of Israel. Old grandpa Isaac had lived for 180 years. He was very old. Isaac didn't mind dying because he said, "I have had a good life."

Jacob and Esau cried anyway. Jacob cried because he remembered how he had hurt his father with the things he had done. Still, Jacob was glad he'd had a chance to say, "I'm sorry." He was glad he had told his father how much he loved him.

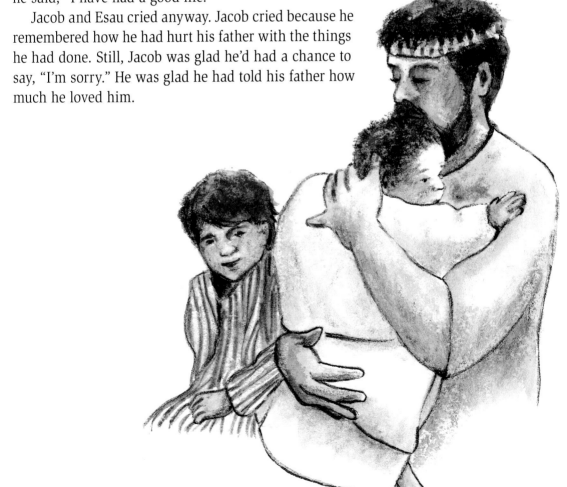

A Child Helps Jesus

BASED ON MATTHEW 14:13–21, MARK 6:31–44,
LUKE 9:10–17, JOHN 6:1–13

Jesus needed a rest.

"Let's go off by ourselves," Jesus said to his special friends, the disciples. "I'm tired. I need to get away from all these people."

So Jesus and his disciples got into a boat. They rowed right across a lake.

But the people followed Jesus anyway. They wanted to hear Jesus tell them how to grow in God's way. A whole crowd of people ran around the edge of lake. Instead of being alone, Jesus and his friends still had a big crowd with them.

Jesus was tired. But he felt sorry for the people. They reminded him of sheep that needed a shepherd to look after them. So Jesus sat down and talked to them about God's love.

"It's getting late," said Philip, one of the disciples. "We should tell the people to go home so they can get something to eat."

"Why don't you give them something to eat, Philip?" Jesus asked.

"There are thousands of people here," said Philip. "We're way out in the country. There's no place to buy food. And we don't have money."

One of the children in the crowd heard Jesus and his friends talking. "I have something we could eat," the boy said to Andrew.

"What have you got?" asked Andrew.

"Five loaves of bread," said the boy. "And two small fish."

Andrew laughed. "Look at all these people! How many could you feed with five loaves of bread and two tiny fish?"

The boy felt sad. He knew it wasn't much, but he wanted to share.

"Have the people sit down on the grass," Jesus said. Then he smiled at the boy. "It's very kind of you to share your food. Let's say thank you to God. Then we can eat."

The disciples handed out the food. Everyone ate as much as they wanted. When all the people were full, there was still lots of food left over.

"How did that happen?" the boy asked.

Jesus smiled. "When people are willing to share, there's always enough for everyone. Thank you for showing us how to share."

Joseph's Beautiful Coat

BASED ON GENESIS 37

Jacob and Leah and their family – in other words, the people of Israel – settled down in the land of Canaan.

They had many animals to look after. Jacob and Leah's 12 sons had to take the animals to many different places to find grass.

Well, not all of the 12 sons.

Joseph, the first baby that Rachel had, was his dad's favourite. Jacob always treated Joseph best of all. The other brothers didn't like that one bit.

Joseph wasn't always very kind to his brothers either. Jacob gave Joseph a very nice coat. It had pretty colours and long sleeves. It was much nicer than the clothes the other brothers had. Sometimes Joseph would show off his fancy coat, just to get his brothers angry.

Joseph had dreams, and he loved to tell his brothers all about them. He loved thinking of what the dreams meant. In those days, people thought dreams could tell you what was going to happen.

"Guess what I dreamed last night?" Joseph said one day. "I dreamed we were working out in the field tying bundles of grain together. All your bundles came and bowed down to my bundle."

"I suppose," snapped one of the brothers, "that means someday you are going to be our boss."

"That's right," laughed Joseph.

Joseph even made his father angry. "I had a dream in which the sun and the moon and 11 stars bowed down to me."

"Are you trying to tell us that you will be the boss over me and your mother and all your brothers?" Jacob growled.

One day, all the brothers except Joseph had taken the animals far away from home to find grass. They had been gone for a long time. Old Jacob worried about them.

"Go and find your brothers," Jacob said to Joseph. "Find out if they're all right. Then come back and tell me."

It was a long walk for Joseph to find his brothers. When they saw him coming in his bright new coat, they felt angry.

"Here comes that dreamer," they said. "He thinks he's so smart. Let's fix him."

So the brothers grabbed Joseph and tore off his fancy coat. Then they threw him into a deep hole. Some of the brothers wanted to kill Joseph. Reuben, the oldest brother, said, "No!"

Just then, they saw some people coming along. They were traders, people who buy things from one person and sell them to somebody else. The traders even sold slaves.

A slave is a person who belongs to somebody, the way you might own a dog or a cat.

So the brothers went up to the traders and said, "Would you like to buy a slave? Cheap?"

They sold Joseph to the traders, who took him to a faraway country called Egypt.

"Now what will we tell Father?" the brothers wondered.

"Let's tell Father that a wild animal killed Joseph," said one of them. So they killed one of their sheep and put the blood all over Joseph's coat. Then they tore holes in the coat.

When they got back home, they showed Joseph's torn and bloody coat to Jacob.

Old Jacob just cried and cried and cried. Nothing the brothers did could make Jacob stop crying. The brothers knew they had done a terrible thing.

God Speaks in a Whisper

BASED ON 1 KINGS 19:9–18

King Ahab was still trying to kill God's prophets. Jezebel, King Ahab's wife, sent some of her servants to find Elijah and kill him. Elijah was afraid.

"Oh, God," said Elijah. "Everything is going wrong. The people of Israel are turning away from you. They are helping King Ahab and Jezebel kill your prophets. I am the only prophet left. Why don't you just kill me, too?"

So God said to Elijah, "Go up to the top of the mountain, and I will speak to you there."

So Elijah went up the mountain. He listened for God's voice.

Elijah heard a strong wind that even blew the rocks around.

But the voice of God was not in the wind.

Elijah felt a mighty earthquake.

But the voice of God was not in the earthquake.

Elijah heard the crackling of a huge fire.

But the voice of God was not in the fire.

Elijah heard a soft, quiet whisper.

God spoke to Elijah in a whisper.

When Elijah heard God's voice, he felt strong enough to keep on being a prophet.

Peter Walks on the Water

BASED ON MATTHEW 14:22–33

Jesus was very tired. People came to Jesus the whole day. Some wanted to hear stories about God's shalom. Others were sick and hoped that Jesus would help them feel better.

At the end of the day, Jesus said to his friends, his disciples, "You take the boat and go to the other side of the lake. I want to go up into the hills for a little while. I need some time to rest. I need to talk with God."

So the disciples started to row across the lake. But a big storm began to blow. A strong wind blew the waves. The waves bounced the boat up and down, and splashed water into the boat.

"We're going to drown!" yelled Andrew. All night long, the storm kept blowing harder and harder. The waves got bigger and bigger. The disciples were shivering because they were so afraid.

And then, when it was almost morning, Andrew saw something that looked like a person walking on the water. "It's a ghost!" screamed Andrew. The other disciples made strange, fearful noises.

Slowly, the person came closer. And closer. Then they saw that it was a man. And as the man came even closer, Andrew knew who it was. "It's Jesus!" he yelled.

"It's all right!" called Jesus. "It's me. Don't be afraid."

"But…but…" Peter could hardly talk. "Jesus, you're…you're…you're walking on the water." Jesus just nodded and smiled.

"Could I walk on the water, too?" asked Peter.

Jesus reached out his hand. "Come, Peter," he said.

So Peter stepped out of the boat. He was looking right at Jesus and that made him feel strong. And sure enough, he could walk on the water, just like Jesus.

Peter didn't look at the waves and he didn't worry about the wind. Peter kept his eyes on Jesus. Step by step. Peter was not afraid.

Then, suddenly, Peter noticed the big waves. Right away he felt afraid. He began to sink into the water. "Help me! Jesus!" he yelled.

Jesus reached out his hand to Peter. Peter grabbed Jesus' hand, and right away he felt strong again.

"Let's get into the boat," said Jesus. And as Peter climbed in, he noticed that the storm was over. The wind and the waves had stopped. The water was calm.

Jesus' friends just sat there in the boat. They didn't know what to say. Andrew wondered if maybe it had all been a dream.

Peter looked right at Jesus. "You really are God's chosen one, aren't you, Jesus?"

PROPER 15 [20]

Joseph Helps the Pharaoh

BASED ON GENESIS 40 – 41

Note to leaders: *This story is not included in the lectionary, but is included here to help children understand the stories that follow.*

It was a terrible time for Joseph. His brothers had sold him, just like you might sell a cow or a horse.

The people who bought Joseph made him walk. Day after day. Joseph often cried. He wanted to be near his father. He wanted to be home. Joseph was tired and hungry. But the people who bought him just made him walk and walk. Day after day. Day after day.

They took Joseph to Egypt. The people in Egypt made him work very hard. But, one day, something wonderful happened.

The pharaoh of Egypt (a pharaoh is like a king) heard that Joseph knew about dreams. The pharaoh had some bad dreams. "Tell me what my dreams mean!" said the pharaoh.

"For seven years, all the plants and all the animals will grow very well. There will be lots of food to eat. There will be *more* food than you can eat.

"After that, for seven years, there will be hardly any food. There will be a famine. The plants and animals won't grow because there will be no rain."

"What should I do?" asked the pharaoh.

"Tell people to save their food during the seven good years. Then they will have food to eat during the seven bad years."

"What a good idea!" said the pharaoh. "And I need you to help me. Will you help the people save enough food during the good years?"

"Yes," said Joseph. "I would be glad to help."

And so Joseph became a very important person. He became one of the most important people in all the land of Egypt.

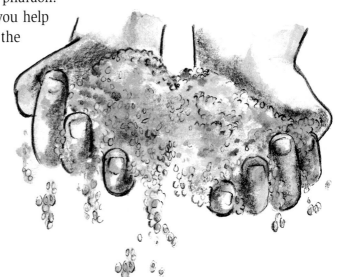

Joseph and His Brothers

BASED ON GENESIS 42 – 45

The famine was happening all over. Joseph and the people of Egypt had enough to eat. But in other countries people were starving.

Far away, in Canaan, Joseph's brothers and sisters and his father Jacob had hardly anything to eat.

One day, Jacob said to his sons, "I hear there's lots of food in Egypt. Take some of the donkeys and go to Egypt to see if you can buy some."

So ten of the brothers left for Egypt. Benjamin didn't go because he was the youngest. His father, Jacob, worried that Benjamin might get hurt on such a long trip.

When the brothers got to Egypt, they asked, "Where can we buy food?"

"Go see the person who takes care of all the food," they were told.

Of course, the brothers didn't know that was Joseph. When they had sold Joseph to the traders many years before that, they didn't think they would ever see him again.

Joseph knew his brothers right away. Joseph was very surprised, but he didn't say anything.

He was glad to see his brothers. But Joseph was still angry at them for selling him to the traders. Joseph felt both angry *and* happy. He was all mixed up inside.

"I think you are spies," Joseph said.

"Oh, no," said the brothers. "We're just ten brothers who have come to buy food. We're not spies."

"If you are brothers, what is your father's name?"

"Our father's name is Jacob. He is living in Canaan."

Joseph was so happy to hear that his father was still alive. He had to stop talking for a while, and he turned away from his brothers. He didn't want them to see the tears in his eyes.

"Are there other members of your family?" Joseph asked.

"There is one more brother, Benjamin. But he was too young to come with us."

"Any others?" Joseph was feeling angry now.

"Well, no. There was another brother, but he died."

"What do you mean, he died?" Joseph was very angry.

The brothers just stood there. They didn't know what to say. They were afraid to say they had sold their brother as a slave.

Joseph could see from the faces of his brothers that they were very sorry for what they had done.

"I am Joseph, your brother," he said.

The brothers couldn't believe it at first. It didn't seem possible. Then they felt afraid. "If this really is Joseph," they thought, "he will be very angry at us for what we did to him."

"Don't be afraid," said Joseph. "I think God wanted me to be in Egypt. God wanted me to help people so they wouldn't starve."

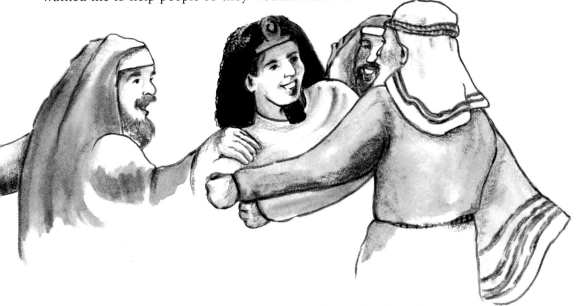

"Thank God," said Reuben, the oldest brother. "Thank God!"

Then the brothers started hugging Joseph and Joseph was hugging them and they were hugging each other. All of them were crying.

Finally Joseph blew his nose and said, "Go back to Canaan. Bring Father and Benjamin and the whole family here to Egypt. I know a nice place where you can live. And there's lots of food here in Egypt."

When the brothers had told Jacob for the 20th time about Joseph in Egypt, the old man finally believed them. Suddenly he looked as if he was 20 years younger.

"Well," said Jacob. "What are we waiting for? Don't just stand around. Let's go."

As Jacob and all his family left Canaan, God came and repeated the promise. "Israel will become a great nation," said God. "And you will come back again to live in your own country."

That is how the people called "Israel" came to be living in Egypt.

A Woman Teaches Jesus

BASED ON MATTHEW 15:21–28

It was so hard for Jesus to find a place to rest. Everywhere he went, people followed him.

One day, Peter said, "Why don't we go to Canaan? It's a different country so people won't know you. You could rest there."

They went to a friend's little house in Canaan. "Go inside and rest," said Peter. "I'll stay out here to make sure nobody bothers you."

Jesus was just lying down for a nap when he heard some noise outside.

"You can't go in there," yelled Peter.

"Well, I am going in there whether you like it or not."

"I said, you can't go in there, woman," Peter yelled again.

"I am going in, mister," said the woman. "I have a sick daughter at home. I am going in there and that prophet of yours is going to fix her. Now get out of my way before I kick you."

Peter jumped aside. The fierce eyes of the woman made him afraid. He followed her into the house. "I told her you wanted to rest, Jesus. But she wouldn't listen."

"Jesus? That is your name?" said the woman. "They say you are a prophet. They say you are a very powerful prophet. Some say you are God's chosen one.

"All right, Jesus. I'm asking you..." Now there were tears in her eyes. "No, I'm begging you, Jesus, Lord, son of David, help my daughter. She is very, very sick. If you don't help her, she will die."

Jesus was sitting on a mat in a corner of the room. He was so tired. He didn't want to talk to anyone. He kept his eyes closed, hoping the woman would go away.

When Jesus didn't say anything, the woman began to yell again. "Look, I'm sorry. But I need your help, Jesus. My daughter is dying and *I need your help*!"

"I can't help you. I'm sorry. That's just the way it is. I was sent to the people of Israel. To the Jews. Not to the people of Canaan. Please go away." Jesus talked very quietly because he was so tired. "I need time to think. I need time to rest."

But the woman would not go away. "If you are God's chosen one, didn't you come to help *all* of God's people?"

"I was sent to help the Jewish people of Israel," said Jesus. "Try to understand. Suppose you are at a table and you have bread there for your family to eat. There is just enough bread for the children. So you don't take the children's bread and give it to the dogs, do you? The Jewish people, the people of Israel, are like the children at that table. And I only have enough bread to feed *them*."

"Right," said the woman. "But even the dogs that run around on the street get to eat some of the bits that fall off the table. Don't you have even a little love to give – a little love for those of us who are not Jewish?"

Jesus rubbed his forehead. He had a headache. Then he remembered the stories he heard when he was just a boy. He remembered the funny story of Jonah. Jonah was sent to tell the people of Ninevah about God. They were not Jewish. He remembered the story of brave Ruth, who came from Moab. She wasn't Jewish, but she became the great, great-grandmother of King David. Then Jesus smiled just a little as he remembered the stories his mom had told him, about the three strangers from a faraway country – the three Magi. And they brought special gifts to him when he was a baby.

"You are right," said Jesus. His voice was just a whisper. "Of course you are right. You are also very brave. Go home. Your daughter will get well. And thank you for coming. You've given me a lot to think about."

"Thank you," said the woman. She walked over and put her hand on Jesus' shoulder. "You need to rest before you can think," she said gently. "I will send you some tea to drink that will help you sleep."

Miriam Saves Her Brother

BASED ON EXODUS 1 – 2

The people of the house of Israel did not go back to Canaan. About 400 years had passed since the time of Joseph. Over those years, the people of Israel began to call themselves "Hebrews." The Hebrew people had kept on living in Egypt because they liked it there. There was lots of food.

But after 400 years most of the Hebrew people had become slaves. They had to work for the Egyptians. But there got to be more and more Hebrews. The Egyptians began to be afraid.

"Those Hebrews!" grumped the pharaoh. "Soon there will be more Hebrews than Egyptians. Why doesn't somebody do something?"

"Sir," said one of the helpers. "You are the pharaoh, the king of Egypt. Could you do something?"

"I guess so," said Pharaoh. He talked to Shiphrah and Puah. They were midwives, women who help when mothers are having babies.

"When one of the Hebrew women has a baby boy," Pha-raoh said, "I want you to kill it."

Shiphrah and Puah could hardly believe that someone would ask for such a terrible thing. So they made a plan.

"Let's tell the pharaoh how strong the Hebrew women are," said Puah. "Let's say they don't need us to help the babies be born."

"Their babies are born before we get there," Shiphrah told the pharaoh.

This was a very brave thing for the two midwives to do. If the pharaoh had found out, he might have killed them. But the pharaoh believed what Shiphrah and Puah said.

So the pharaoh tried something else. He gave an order: "When a boy baby is born, throw it in the river and drown it." The pharaoh sent his soldiers to look in all the houses to make sure all the baby boys were drowned.

The Hebrew people tried everything to keep their babies away from the pharaoh's soldiers. But usually the soldiers found the babies anyway.

When a woman named Jochebed gave birth to a baby boy, she and her husband Amram didn't know what to do. They kept the baby hidden for a while. But as the baby grew it was noisy sometimes. They knew the soldiers would find the baby and kill it.

One day, Jochebed and the baby's older sister, Miriam, had an idea. They made a special basket for the baby. They fixed the basket so it would float on water.

Then Jochebed and Miriam took the basket to the edge of the river. They put the basket in the water among the reeds. "The soldiers will never find the baby here," said Jochebed. "Miriam, please stay close by so nothing bad happens to the baby."

Imagine Miriam's surprise when she saw a princess come down to the river. It was the pharaoh's daughter coming to have a bath.

Now Miriam was really worried. "If the princess sees the basket with the baby, she'll call the soldiers. They will kill my baby brother."

Sure enough, the princess saw the basket. She sent one of her helpers to get it for her.

"Oh, what a beautiful baby," said the princess. The little baby was crying, so the princess picked it up and cuddled it. "I'm going to take care of this baby as if he were my very own."

When Miriam heard that, she had another good idea. She ran over to the princess and said, "Would you like me to find someone who can feed the baby milk from her breasts and take very good care of it for you?"

"Why, yes!" said the princess.

So Miriam ran and got Jochebed, her mother.

"Take this baby, and take good care of him," the princess told Jochebed. "I will pay you for your work."

Later in the day, Miriam and her mother were talking about what had happened. Miriam jumped up and down and squealed, she was so happy.

"Shhh," said her mother. "People will hear you."

But Jochebed couldn't keep from laughing. "All I wanted was to keep my baby from being killed by the pharaoh. Now the pharaoh's daughter is paying me to look after my own little baby. I think God must have some plans for this child."

When the baby got a little older, the princess took the baby to the palace to live.

"I will raise him as if he is an Egyptian," said the princess. "He will live like a prince in the pharaoh's palace. And I will call him Moses, which means, 'I lifted him out of the water.'"

Simon Becomes Peter

BASED ON MATTHEW 16:13–23

Simon was mixed up. He had been following Jesus for many months. Simon had listened very carefully when Jesus talked. He tried so hard to understand. But often Simon just didn't know what Jesus was talking about.

Simon was one of Jesus' special friends. A disciple.

Jesus often sat with the disciples and talked to them about God. It was like going to school. Or church.

Simon didn't really like this kind of school. "I feel so stupid," he told Jesus one day. "You explain things. Everybody else knows what you mean. But I don't!"

"What don't you understand, Simon?" asked Jesus.

"Well, I've been trying to figure out who you are. Are you a prophet? Are you a teacher? Are you a doctor?"

"Let's see what the others think," said Jesus. Jesus asked all his friends to sit down under an olive tree with him. "Now tell me," said Jesus. "When you are talking to the people who gather around – who do people say I am?"

"Some say you are John the Baptizer."

"I heard someone say, 'Jesus is really the prophet Elijah come back to life.'"

"And I've heard people say you are the prophet Jeremiah."

Each of the disciples had heard something different.

Jesus was laughing. "Well, I can't be all those people. Who do *you* think I am?"

Simon's face lit up. He had a new idea. "I know. I know. You are the Christ. You are the Messiah. You are the one God is sending to show us how much God loves us." Simon was very excited.

Jesus was quiet for a long time. He looked at his friends. Then he looked hard at Simon.

"Simon. My friend. God gave you that new idea. You didn't get that idea all by yourself. It's a big idea. It's a hard idea. Your idea is like a big, hard, solid rock.

"So I am going to give you a new name. Your name will not be Simon anymore. It will be Peter. Peter means 'rock.' This idea, Peter, this big rock of an idea, will never go away. All my friends, all the people who follow me in God's way, will remember your idea. Always. It will be like a solid rock they can stand on.

"But for now," said Jesus, "this has to be our secret. The crowds that come to hear me wouldn't understand."

Moses Kills a Man

BASED ON EXODUS 2:11–25

Note to leaders: This story does not appear in the lectionary, but is included here so children can better understand the lectionary story that follows.

Moses liked living in the pharaoh's palace, most of the time. But sometimes somebody in the palace got angry at him. Or the princess got annoyed. Then they called him a "Hebrew."

As he grew older, Moses realized that Hebrews were people who worked as slaves for the pharaoh. The Egyptians usually treated the Hebrew people like animals.

As Moses grew up, he really wanted to learn more about the Hebrew people. "They are *my* people," he said to himself. Moses even wanted to find out who his real mom and dad were. He could barely remember them.

It didn't take Moses long to find his family. He had some wonderful evenings talking with his mother, Jochebed, his sister, Miriam, his father, Amram, and his brother, Aaron.

They told Moses about the brave midwives. They told him how they made a basket for him, to float on the water. They told how Pharaoh's daughter found him. They laughed about how Miriam offered to find someone to look after the baby.

They also told Moses about an old, old promise that God had made to the Hebrew people. They told Moses about Abraham and Sarah, about Isaac and Leah and Rachel, and about Joseph and his brothers.

Moses felt very mixed up sometimes. "I live like a prince in a palace," he thought. "The princess treats me like a son. But my people are slaves! Who am I, anyway?"

Moses often went to the places where the Hebrew slaves worked. They had to make big buildings for the pharaoh. Moses noticed that the Hebrew slaves didn't have enough food to eat. Their bodies were covered with sores.

Sometimes the Hebrew slaves were too sick to work. Then the bosses would beat them with whips. Moses felt angry.

One day, Moses saw one of the bosses beating a worker who could hardly stand up. "Please don't hit me anymore," cried the worker. "I just can't stand up. My legs hurt so much."

"You're just lazy," yelled the boss beating the worker some more. "Get up and get to work!"

Moses got very angry. He hit the boss hard and killed him.

Moses knew he was in trouble. He ran away, out of the city and into the hills. He ran all the way to a place called Midian.

Moses felt tired. When he came to a well, he had a big drink of cold water and sat down to rest. While he sat there, seven sisters came by. They began giving their flock of sheep a drink.

Just then, other shepherds came along and chased the seven sisters away. Moses got angry again. "The seven sisters were here first!" yelled Moses, and he chased the other shepherds away.

The sisters wanted to say "thank you" to Moses. They invited him to come for supper. As it turned out, Moses got along very well with the seven sisters, and with their mother and father. They asked Moses to stay with them.

After a while, Moses and Zipporah, one of the seven sisters, got married. Sometime later they had a baby.

Moses was very happy with his new family. But even so, he remembered his home in Egypt. He thought about his own Hebrew people. Moses worried about how the pharaoh was treating them.

Most of all, he thought about his mother, Jochebed, and his sister, Miriam. Moses thought about the princess who had adopted him. He thought about the midwives who wouldn't kill the babies, even though the pharaoh told them to.

"Those women must really have been living in God's way," he thought. "If it hadn't been for them, I wouldn't be alive."

Moses Goes Back to Egypt

BASED ON EXODUS 3 – 4

Back in Egypt, things were worse for the Hebrew people. The pharaoh who wanted to kill Moses had died.

The new pharaoh made the Hebrew people work even harder. Moses often thought about them.

One day, out in the hills, Moses saw something very strange. It was a bush on fire. Moses didn't know why a bush should be burning all by itself out there in the hills.

Moses went a little closer. He saw that even though the bush was on fire, it wasn't getting burned up. The bush just kept burning and burning. "I'd better go even closer to see this," said Moses.

Then Moses heard a voice. "Moses! Moses!"

Moses was afraid. "Yes?" he said. "Here I am."

"Don't come any closer, Moses," said the voice. "And take off your shoes. You are standing on holy ground."

Moses was even more afraid now. He didn't run away, but he took off his shoes quickly. "Maybe it's God talking to me," he thought.

"I am the God of your great, great, grandparents," said the voice. "I am the God who gave the promise to Abraham and Sarah. I am the God of Isaac and Rebecca."

Moses covered his face with his hands. Now he was very afraid.

"Moses," the voice said, "I have heard the cry of the Hebrew people in Egypt. I know how much they are hurting. I want to take them out of Egypt and send them back to the land they came from – to Canaan. And Moses, I am sending you to lead them out of Egypt."

"Yes but, God," said Moses, "I don't know how to do that."

"I will be with you, Moses. I will help you."

"Yes, but," said Moses, "what if they ask me your name? What should I tell them?"

"Moses," said God, "I am who I am. If they want to know who sent you, say I AM sent you."

"Yes, but," Moses said again, "I don't know how to talk very well. When I try to say things, my words get all mixed up. Can't you send somebody else?"

"Moses! No more yes-buts." God seemed to be getting angry at Moses. "If you need someone to talk for you, ask your brother, Aaron. Aaron is already on his way to meet you, to ask you to help your people. Just remember. I will be with you. Now go!"

Moses didn't want to go. He was afraid to go.

But Moses went. Moses believed that God would be with him.

Moses and his wife, Zipporah, and their baby began the long walk back to Egypt. Along the way, sure enough, his brother, Aaron, was coming toward him. They gave each other a hug and a kiss and sat down to talk.

"Pharaoh is making our people work harder," said Aaron. "They don't have enough food. Many of them are sick."

Moses told Aaron about the burning bush and about what God had told him to do.

So Moses and Aaron went back to Egypt. They had a big meeting with all the Hebrew people.

"God really cares about how much you are hurting," said Aaron to all the people. "And God will help us get away from Pharaoh."

Going to School

BASED ON MATTHEW 16:21–26

"There's so much to learn!" Mary of Magdala said to Jesus one day. "You are teaching us so many things about helping and caring and loving. It's hard, sometimes, to be your friend."

"That's right," said Jesus. "And I won't always be here to teach you."

"That's the part I don't like," said Peter.

"What do you mean, Peter?" asked Mary.

"I don't like it when Jesus talks about leaving us!"

"That's why I am teaching you these things, Peter. When the time comes, and I must leave you, you will be ready."

Peter was almost ready to cry. He stood up and walked away from where the other disciples were sitting. He found a rock to sit down on. Peter just wanted to be by himself for a little while.

Mary and Jesus and the others kept talking for a while. Then Jesus got up and walked to where Peter was sitting. He put his hand on Peter's shoulder.

Peter looked up at Jesus. "Why do you have to say that, Jesus?" Peter said. "I hate it when you talk about going to Jerusalem. I hate it when you say that people there might take you and kill you. I hate it!"

That night, Jesus and his friends sat around their campfire. They had some fish and some bread to eat. But they didn't talk very much.

"Try not to be afraid," Jesus said to the disciples. "I know that's hard, but please try. Because some bad things are going to happen. I don't know exactly what those bad things are. But I know I have to go to Jerusalem, and I know the rulers there are afraid of me. So they will try to hurt me."

Mary stood up and put some more sticks of wood on the fire. The light from the fire showed the tears in her eyes.

"I am asking you to do a hard thing," said Jesus. "I want you to leave your families – to leave your friends. I am asking you to leave all those things behind, and come and follow me. It will be hard and you will cry. But if you do this, you will find something much more wonderful."

Jesus sat quietly for a while. None of the disciples said anything. They were thinking about what Jesus had said.

"Here's a really hard thing to understand," said Jesus. He was smiling now. "If you try to hold on to the good things in your life, you will lose them. But if you lose them, you will find new things in your life that are much better."

"I still don't understand," said Peter.

"I know," said Jesus. "But think about what I have said. Think about it over and over. It may take a long time, but you will understand."

The Hebrews Leave Egypt

BASED ON EXODUS 5 – 12

The Hebrew people all cheered when Moses and Aaron spoke to them. They hated being slaves. They wanted to be free.

So the brothers went to the palace to talk to the pharaoh.

"God wants you to let our people go," they said.

The pharaoh was very angry. "I will not let your people go. They belong to me. Tell your people to get back to work."

The pharaoh was so angry, he made things even harder for the Hebrew slaves. They had to make bricks for the pharaoh's big buildings. They made the bricks out of clay and straw.

Now the pharaoh told them, "You have to get your own straw. Go out into the fields to find it. But you have to make just as many bricks as before." The pharaoh told his bosses to beat the people if they didn't make enough bricks.

Then the Hebrew people were angry at Moses and Aaron. "You ask the pharaoh to let us go. What happens? We have to work harder. You make things worse. Why don't you just go away and mind your own business?"

Moses was upset. "Is this why you sent me here?" he said to God. "Now the pharaoh makes people work harder. You made things worse!"

"Moses," God said, "I made a promise to Abraham and Sarah and to all their children's children. I made a promise that you will be a great nation. Go and tell that to my people."

So Moses talked to the Hebrew people. "Remember God's promise," he said. "Please trust God. It's very important."

Some of the people believed Moses. Others didn't.

God helped Moses and Aaron try to make the pharaoh let the people go. God turned the river into blood. Zillions of frogs and bugs and flies came. The cows and sheep got sick and there were sores on the people. There was hail and grass-hoppers. One time it turned dark in the middle of the day. These things only happened to the Egyptians, not to the Hebrew people.

But Pharaoh would not let the Hebrew people go.

Then God said to Moses and Aaron, "I will do one more thing to the pharaoh and to the Egyptians. Then they will let my people go."

So God told Moses exactly what was going to happen. Moses had to explain it to the Hebrew people.

"Listen carefully," Moses said. "I want you all to get ready. We are going to leave Egypt. But tonight I want you to have a very special meal.

"Kill a small goat or a sheep, and roast it. Take some of the blood from the goat or sheep. Smear it on your front door. That way God will know which houses are Hebrew and which are Egyptian."

That night the Hebrew people ate the roasted sheep. They smeared the blood on their front doors. Many of the people said prayers to God.

God made a sickness come into the homes of all the Egyptians. The oldest child in every house died. Even the pharaoh's oldest child died.

But none of the Hebrew children died. And the people said, "The sickness passed over our homes because we had put the blood on our doors."

That same night all the Egyptians, especially the pharaoh, wanted the Hebrew slaves to leave. "Get out," they yelled. "Get out quickly. Take anything you want, just go."

The Hebrew people left quickly.

It was like a whole city full of people all walking out together. Many of them had started making bread. They had to leave so quickly, they didn't have time to let the bread get soft. They picked everything up and left.

Miriam was walking with her two brothers, Moses and Aaron. "We will never forget this time," she said to them. "My people will always remember how God was with us. We will never forget God's promise."

"We will never forget," said Moses.

And the Hebrew people still remember this time every year. They remember what God did for them many, many years ago.

They celebrate with a special meal. They tell the story of how the Hebrew people were freed from being slaves. They eat food like hard bread that reminds them of what happened.

They call that celebration "Passover," because they remember how the terrible sickness passed over their homes and their children.

How to Fix a Problem

BASED ON MATTHEW 18:15–20

Every day, there were many people who came
to listen to Jesus. They wanted to hear his parables about God. They wanted to learn how to
live God's way.

In the evenings, when all the people had
gone to their homes, Jesus and his friends
would cook some food on a campfire. They
didn't have very much money to buy food.
Sometimes there wasn't enough to feed
them all.

One evening, they cooked a pot of stew
on the campfire. When it was ready, each
one put some of the food onto their own
plate.

"Susanna!" Andrew sounded angry.

"What?" said Susanna.

"You're doing it again! You're taking
more than your share."

"Mind your own business!" said Susanna. "I'm hungry!"

"So am I," said Andrew. "We're all hungry. But you shouldn't take more than your
share of the food. You've been doing
that every night. It's not fair!"

Andrew and Susanna both sat
down. Both of them looked angry and
hurt. Neither of them said anything for the rest of the meal. Everyone felt unhappy.

"Susanna and Andrew are angry at each other," Mary said to Jesus. "That's
not living God's way, is it?"

"No," said Jesus. "And I think there could be a better way to fix this kind of a
problem. Andrew? When did you first see Susanna take more than her share of
the food?"

"Two days ago," said Andrew.

"Think about this," said Jesus. "Suppose you talked to Susanna when nobody else was nearby. Suppose you spoke very gently and said, 'Susanna, I think you took more than your share of the food.'"

"That's right," said Susanna. "He didn't have to say it so all my friends could hear."

"But suppose I did that," said Andrew, "and Susanna still kept taking more than her share of the food?"

"Then it might help if you talked to two other people. Maybe two of the people who are really good friends of Susanna's. You could say to them, 'I have a problem. Susanna is taking more than her share of the food. I talked to her about it, but she still keeps taking more. Would you come with me so that all three of us can ask her to stop doing that?'"

"Sure," said Andrew. "But what if she still wouldn't stop taking more than her share?"

"Andrew," said Jesus. "Susanna is good person. I think she would say, 'I'm sorry. I won't do that anymore.' Then you could give her a hug and say to her, 'We love you and God loves you.'"

"Yeah, but what if…what if she still keeps taking more than her share?"

"Then you have to talk about it with the whole group of friends," Andrew. "But not the way you did it just now."

"What should I say?" Andrews looked very puzzled.

"First of all, you should only do this when Susanna is there with you. You should never talk about a person when they can't hear you.

"Then you speak very gently to all the friends. You could say, 'I have a problem. Each time we eat together, I see Susanna taking more than her share of the food. I talked with her about it. I took two other friends to talk with her about it. But she keeps doing it.' When you have said that, then you ask Susanna if she would like to say something."

Then Jesus looked at Susanna. "Would you like to say something right now, Susanna?"

Susanna sat very quietly just looking at the ground.

"Well, I think she…" Andrew started to talk, but Jesus held up his hand to tell him to not say anything. "Give Susanna time to think of what she wants to say," said Jesus.

Everyone sat quietly for a while. Then Susanna looked up. "I'm sorry," she said. "I know all of us would like more food. I was being selfish. I'm sorry. I'll try not to do that anymore."

Everybody was quiet. Then Andrew walked over to where Susanna was sitting. "May I give you a hug?" he asked her. Susanna stood up. She and Andrew gave each other a hug.

"Do you forgive me?" she asked Andrew.

"Sure," said Andrew. "We all forgive you. And God forgives you, too."

"Wonderful!" said Jesus. "Now there's one more thing to remember. We don't talk about this anymore. And we don't keep watching to see how much food Susanna puts on her plate. We had a problem. We fixed it. And that's that! We've learned that God loves and forgives every one of us."

A Long, Long Journey

BASED ON EXODUS 14 – 15

Miriam and her brothers and all the Hebrew people began a long, long journey. It was a journey that would last for 40 years. Many things happened to them on this journey.

The first thing was that the pharaoh changed his mind. Again.

The Hebrew people were camping beside the sea. They didn't know how to get to the other side. Then, off in the distance, someone saw the pharaoh's soldiers coming. Hundreds of them, with their horses and their sharp swords.

"What are we going to do?" the people said to Moses. "Did you have to drag us all the way out here in the desert? You've made things worse again. Now the pharaoh's soldiers will kill us."

Once again, God saved the Hebrews. A strong wind blew the water away so the Hebrews could walk through to the other side of the sea. They had to walk fast because the pharaoh's army was right behind them. When all the Hebrews were on the other side, the wind stopped. The water came back. The pharaoh's soldiers drowned.

When all the Hebrew people were safe again, they decided to have a celebration. A party. They wanted to say "thank you" to God for saving them.

Moses and the people sang a long song.

Then Miriam gathered all the women together. Miriam was a prophet. A prophet is a leader who helps people understand how to live in God's way.

Miriam beat her little drum. She and all the women danced. It was a happy dance. And Miriam sang a song.

Sing a song to God
for God has done great things.
God has thrown the horse and rider
down into the sea.

Then everybody joined in the dancing and singing.
"Were not slaves anymore," they shouted. "We are free! Thank you, God!"

Over and Over and Over and Over

BASED ON MATTHEW 18:21–22

Susanna sat quietly. She was thinking.

The rest of Jesus' disciples were talking and laughing as they sat around the campfire after supper. But Susanna was remembering when she took more than her share of the food. She remembered how Andrew and the others had said, "We forgive you!"

"Jesus?" she said. "How often should we forgive someone? I mean, if someone keeps doing something bad, should we just say, 'I forgive you!' over and over?"

"Sure!" said Jesus. "Over and over and over and over."

"But what if someone keeps doing something they shouldn't do?" Susanna asked.

"You have a baby brother, don't you?"

"Yes," said Susanna. "He's almost two years old. His name is Alphaeus. We call him Alfie for short."

"Now suppose Alfie wets his clothes. Would you forgive him?

"Of course!" laughed Susanna.

"What else would you do?"

"I'd get him some dry clothes."

"And if he wet his clothes again, would you forgive him?"

"Of course!"

"What if Alfie did it over and over and over and over. How often would you forgive him? How often would you put dry clothes on him?'

"I'd do it over and over and over and over," laughed Susanna. "But, Jesus, Alfie's not even two! He doesn't know he shouldn't wet his clothes."

Jesus smiled. "You know something, Susanna? Most of the time, when people are doing a bad thing, they don't really know it's a bad thing. Often, it's because they don't know how to do good things."

"We're trying to teach Alfie how to keep his clothes dry. He's starting to learn."

"You know something, Susanna? God is a little bit like a big sister. God keeps forgiving us, over and over and over and over. Just like you do with little Alfie. And at the same time, God is helping us learn how to be more kind, more loving. And fair."

PROPER 20 [25]

I'm So Hungry!

BASED ON EXODUS 16:1–15

"It's such a long way," Miriam sighed.

"I know," said Aaron. "It's hot in the daytime and cold at night. And I'm so hungry."

"So am I," said Miriam. "But there's no food anywhere."

The Hebrew people hadn't eaten anything for days. "Why did you drag us into the desert to die?" they said to Moses. "We were slaves in Egypt, but we had enough to eat. We can almost smell the meat cooking. The spices made it taste really good. We are not slaves anymore, but we are so hungry. You want us to die out here in the desert?"

"No, I don't," said Moses. "God doesn't want you to die either. God got us out of Egypt. God will give us food. Trust God! Please!"

Sure enough, in the evening, a whole flock of birds flew into their camp. They were quail, a bird that looks like a small chicken. They make a funny "cwa-ka-koo" kind of noise. When you cook them, they taste really good.

So the people caught the quail and cooked them for food. They said, "Thank you, God, for sending the quail."

The next morning they found some white sticky stuff growing on the plants and on the ground. They called it manna.

"Hmmm! This is good," said Miriam.

"What does it taste like?" asked Aaron.

"Sort of like a biscuit made with honey. I like it."

Moses told the people the manna would come every day. "This is God's bread," he said. "Gather enough for one day. On the sixth day of the week, gather twice as much. Because the seventh day is our Sabbath, God's day of rest. Gather enough for the Sabbath on the sixth day so you can rest on the seventh."

Now the people had enough to eat. They were happy for a little while. Then they started complaining again.

The Kind Farmer

BASED ON MATTHEW 20:1–16

Jesus told his friends many stories.

Here is a parable – a story about God's shalom. Shalom is what happens when people love and help each other, when they try their best to live in God's way. In this story, God is like the farmer.

There was a farmer who had a big field of grapes. The grapes were ripe and juicy.

"My goodness," said the farmer. "These grapes are ready to pick. I can't do this all by myself. I need some help."

So, early in the morning, the farmer went to the town and found some helpers. "Pick the grapes for me, and I'll give you 50 coins."

So the helpers worked hard all morning. But at lunchtime the farmer looked at all the grapes that still needed to be picked. "My goodness! We'll never get all these grapes picked today. I need some more helpers."

So the farmer went back to the town and found some more helpers.

Later in the afternoon, the farmer looked again at all the grapes that still needed to be picked. "My goodness! We'll never get all these grapes picked today. I need some more helpers."

So the farmer went and found even *more* helpers.

At the end of the day, when it was starting to get dark, the farmer said to the helpers, "Come. I'll pay you."

First, the farmer paid the helpers who came late in the afternoon. "Here's 50 coins."

Then the farmer paid the helpers who came at lunchtime. "Here's 50 coins."

And then the farmer paid the helpers who had worked all day. "Here's 50 coins."

"Hey! That's not fair!" said the first helpers. "We picked grapes when it was cold in the morning and when the sun was hot in the afternoon. How come you gave 50 coins to the people who came late in the afternoon? If you gave them 50 coins, you should pay us more!"

"You don't understand," said the farmer. "I promised you 50 coins and I gave you 50 coins. Stop complaining. I like to give my money away to people. Even when they haven't worked very long. Even when they don't deserve it. I give things to people because I love them. That's the kind of farmer I am."

We Want a Drink!

BASED ON EXODUS 17:1–7

The people of Israel had been very hungry. But God had given them a special food called manna, which tasted really good. And God had sent some quail – birds that look like small chickens. They cooked the quail on a fire, and they tasted good, too.

Now the people had enough to eat, but they were thirsty. There was no water anywhere. They started complaining again. "Stop it!" said Moses. "Stop saying that God isn't good to us."

"But we are thirsty! We need water to drink."

"Don't talk like that!" said Moses. "God might get angry if you talk like that!"

"But where is God?" asked the people. "Is God still with us? Why did you drag us out of Egypt just so we would die of thirst here in the desert?" they yelled at Moses. "You've made things worse again! This is a terrible desert. God isn't here in this awful place!"

So Moses asked God, "What am I supposed to do? The people have started to throw stones at me. They are ready to kill me."

God told Moses to walk out into the desert. "Go to a special rock that I will show you. Hit it hard with your walking stick."

"What good will that do?" asked Moses. "Hitting a rock with a stick won't give me water."

"Do it!" said God. So Moses hit the rock with his walking stick. Clean, pure water came running out of the rock.

Then Moses said to the people, "God is with us. Remember that. God is with us. God will never leave us. We are God's people!"

But the people didn't always remember. It's hard to remember that God cares about you, when you are hungry and thirsty and tired and hot and homesick.

The Sister and the Brother

BASED ON MATTHEW 21:28–32

Most people liked to listen to Jesus. They liked to hear him talk about how to be kind and fair to everyone. They liked his parables.

But some of the rulers didn't like him. "People listen to *his* stories," they said. "But they don't listen to the things *we* tell them. Jesus even tells his stories to bad people."

So the rulers went to Jesus. "We don't like your stories. And you shouldn't tell them to bad people."

Jesus smiled at them. "Let me tell you a story," he said. "It's about a family. The mother and the father lived on a farm, where there was a lot of work to do. They had two children. A boy and a girl.

One day, the mother said to the boy, 'We have lots of work to do on the farm today. We have figs to pick from the trees. We have some weeds to pull. And we have chickens to feed. Will you please help us today?"

"Ah," said the boy. "I don't feel like it. I don't like working on the farm. I don't want to help."

So the mother went and talked to his sister. 'We have lots of work to do on the farm today. We have figs to pick. We have some weeds to pull. And we have chickens to feed. Will you please help us today?"

"Sure!" said the girl. "I'd love to help. Just tell me which work I should do first."

"Why don't you feed the chickens first. They're very hungry."

"Okay!" said the girl. But she didn't do it. She started to play. She forgot all about the work she promised to do.

The boy began to play, too. But then he started thinking. "Mother and father have so much work to do. I really should go out and help." So the boy went and fed the chickens and picked the figs and pulled the weeds.

Then Jesus said to the rulers, "You talk a lot about living God's way. But that doesn't help. It doesn't matter much what you *say*. It's what you *do*. I tell my stories to the people you don't like. You say they are bad because they don't say the right words or because their clothes are ragged. But they are kind and gentle to others. They live God's way. *They* are the ones that really listen to my stories."

The Ten Commandments

BASED ON EXODUS 19 – 20

Note to leaders: Another version of this story may be found on page 72.

Three months after God helped the Hebrew people get away from Egypt, they came to a place called Sinai. There was a high mountain in Sinai.

One day, God asked Moses to come up the mountain.

"I want to give you a message for the people of Israel," God said to Moses. "Remember how I brought you out of Egypt? I carried you out like a mother eagle carries her babies. Remember the promises I made to your great, great, great-grandparents? I promised that you would be a great nation. I promised that many years from now people would learn about me because of you. But you must do the things I ask you to do."

So Moses went back and told all the people to gather near the mountain. "God has some very important things to tell us, and we have to be ready to listen carefully. Don't try to come up the mountain with me. Just wait at the bottom. You will be able to hear God's voice."

So the people gathered near the mountain. At the top of the mountain, they could see smoke and fire. They could hear thunder. Everything shook like an earthquake.

Moses went up the mountain, into the smoke and the fire. There God told him ten important things to remember. We call them The Ten Commandments.

I am your God. I brought you out of Egypt, out of the land of slavery. Don't pretend there are any other gods. I am the only one.

Don't make pictures or statues or anything else that you think might look like me. Don't bow down to them or pray to them.

Be careful how you use my name. When you speak my name, you must mean what you are saying.

Remember the Sabbath day, the seventh day of the week. Work on the other six days. Rest on the seventh day and make it a special day.

Treat your mother and your father with respect. Be good to them.

Don't kill anyone.

Don't have sex with anyone you are not married to.

Don't steal.

Don't tell lies about anyone.

Don't wish you had things that belong to other people.

The people were afraid when they saw all the smoke and heard God's voice. But they said "thank you" to God. They were glad to know how to live in God's way.

God's Beautiful Sky

BASED ON PSALM 19:1–6

Look at all that beautiful sky!
It tells us a story of God.
In the daytime, it tells the story in blue;
at night, in the sparkling of stars;
even though there isn't any sound.
We don't hear anyone speak
but the voice of the sky tells a story;
the stars sing a song about God.

God has made us that wonderful sky
and the sun that shines every day.
The sun rides across from the east to the west;
like a bright golden bird it flies.
The sun helps the plants grow strong and tall;
the sun warms our hands and our face.

Keep Your Promise!

BASED ON MATTHEW 21:33–46

Here's another story Jesus told to help us understand God's shalom.

James and his mother had a really nice garden. In their garden, they planted grapevines. The vines grew sweet, dark red grapes that were really good to eat. They called their garden a "vineyard."

But James and his mother had a problem. There was a lot of work to be done in the vineyard. James worked very hard to pull out the weeds. He tied the vines up with strong string so the grapes wouldn't lie on the ground. He chased the birds away so they wouldn't eat his grapes.

But James was only ten years old, so he couldn't work as hard as a grownup. And he had to go to synagogue school, so he didn't have enough time to do the work.

James' mother couldn't help him. She had to cook food and make clothes and take care of his sisters and brothers. There was no father in the family.

"What shall we do?" James asked. "Our vineyard will be spoiled if we don't take care of it!"

"I have an idea," said James' mother. "I know the Jesher family who live not very far from us. Maybe they would like to take care of our vineyard. The Jeshers could keep most of the grapes for themselves, but they would give us some of the grapes, too, because the garden belongs to us."

That sounded like a good idea, so James and his mother went to visit the Jesher family. "Yes, that's a good idea," they said. "We'll take care of your garden, and each year we'll share some of the grapes with you."

But that isn't what happened.

The Jeshers took good care of the vineyard. But they never gave James and his mother any of the grapes. So James' mother sent them a note. "Please give us our share of the grapes," she said.

The Jeshers just tore the note up and threw it on the ground.

"Why don't you go see them," James' mother said. "Remind them that they were going to give us our share of the grapes."

So James went over to the Jeshers, but they just yelled at him and told him to go home. And they had a big black dog that growled at him. When James came home, he was crying.

James' mother was very upset. "I'll go talk to them myself," she said. But the Jeshers did the same thing to her. They yelled at her and told her to go home. And the dog growled at her, too.

But James' mother didn't go home. She stood right there and told the Jeshers, "You can't use our vineyard anymore. You said you would give us our share of the grapes. But you didn't. So we will find someone else to look after our garden. We will find people who will keep their promises."

The People Do a Bad Thing

BASED ON EXODUS 32:1–26

Moses often went up to the top of the mountain. He felt really close to God when he was up there.

It was hard being a leader for the people of Israel. The people walked through the hot desert every day. They shivered in the cold every night. They were tired and cranky.

"Why is Moses up on that mountain so often?" said the people.

"That is where he can talk to God," said Aaron. Aaron was Moses' brother.

"We never get to talk to God," said the people. "We don't really like that God Moses talks about. We want a god we can see. We want a god we can pray to."

"If that's what you want, I can make you a god," said Aaron. "Give me all the gold from your earrings. Give me the gold from the rings on your fingers."

So the people brought all their gold to Aaron. Aaron put it in a very hot fire and melted it. Then he made a statue, shaped like a calf.

"There you are!" said Aaron proudly. "Didn't I make you a beautiful god?"

The people prayed to the golden calf. They sang songs to the golden calf. "This is much better," they said. "This is a god we can see." And they had themselves a big party, with dancing and singing and lots of good food.

Meanwhile, up on the mountain, God was talking to Moses. "Go back down to your people," said God. "Hurry! They are doing a very bad thing. They have made themselves a golden calf and they are praying to it instead of to me!"

"That's terrible," said Moses. "What are you going to do?"

"I'm angry," said God. "Really angry! I'm going to send a hot fire down to burn them up. A very hot fire."

"Please don't!" said Moses. "If you do that, the people in Egypt will laugh. They will say that the people of Israel were not your special chosen people after all. 'Their god got them out into the desert, and then their god burned them up!' That's what the Egyptians will say."

"Well, okay," said God. "But you get down there right now. Tell them to get rid of that golden calf!"

So Moses hurried down. "Aaron!" he yelled. "What is going on? Why are the people praying to a golden calf?"

Aaron looked very guilty. "I don't know," he said. "They just brought me all their gold. I didn't know what to do with it. So I threw it into the fire. And out came this calf."

Moses gathered all the people together. "Listen to me!" he said. "You did a bad thing. Because of that, I have ground up your calf into a powder. I have put that powder into the water you drink. That will make it taste bad. It will make you feel bad. That is your punishment."

"Oh no!" said the people.

"Oh yes!" said Moses. "Now listen to me. Those of you who are sorry for what you did – those of you who want to pray to the real God – you go stand over there. Those who don't want to pray to the real God – well, you can just go away. I don't want to see you anymore!"

Some of the people were really angry at Moses. They liked praying and singing to the golden calf. So they just walked away.

Then Moses turned back to the people who hadn't gone away. "Do you want to pray to the real God? Do you want to pray to the God who brought you out of Egypt? Do you want to pray to the God who gave you food and water in the desert? Do you?"

"Yes, we do!" the people all shouted. "Yes we do!"

"All right. Then right now I want you to pray. Tell God you are sorry for what you did. Then you must promise God not to do bad things again."

And so the people of Israel were very quiet. They were all praying to God. "I'm sorry, God," they said. "I will try very hard to live in your way."

The Best Bar Mitzvah Party

BASED ON MATTHEW 22:1–10

God's shalom is a little like a party. Like a bar mitzvah party for a boy when he becomes 12 years old, or a bat mitzvah party for a girl when she is 12.

Nathanael and his family had planned a really big bar mitzvah party. They worked for many days to prepare a lot of food. It was going to be a really good time.

Then Nathanael and his parents had to decide which people to invite to his party. "We should invite all the important people who live in our town," said Nathanael's father.

"I'd like to invite all the popular kids," said Nathanael. "I'll invite the kids who are the best players whenever we play games together."

"We should invite all the rich families," said Nathanael's mother. "They'll bring good presents."

So Nathanael and his parents sent out all the invitations. They invited the important people, the popular people, the rich people.

On the day of the party, Nathanael was really excited. He and his family were all dressed in their best clothes. The food was all ready. But nobody came to his bar mitzvah. Nobody!

Nathanael and his mother and father were really upset. His father was angry – so angry he could hardly talk. His mother started sweeping the floor really hard, even though it didn't need sweeping.

Then Nathanael had another idea. "If those important people, the popular people, the rich people won't come to my bar mitzvah party, I know some people who will come!"

"Who?" asked his mother.

"The family next door who are very poor. They often don't have enough to eat, and one of their sons, Joshua, is blind. He can never play in any of our games."

Nathanael's mother stopped sweeping. "There are beggars sitting near the marketplace. They would really like the food we have."

Then they both looked at Nathanael's father. They waited quite a while until he was ready to talk. Finally he stood up. "Right! Let's do it!"

So Nathanael and his mother and father invited all the people who hardly ever get invited to parties. "Thank you so much," said Joshua's mother from next door. Then she whispered to Nathanael, "My son has never been to a bar mitzvah party. He's never been to any kind of a party."

And so all the people came to Nathanael's bar mitzvah. They ate and they sang and they laughed and they danced. It was a wonderful party.

When the bar mitzvah party was over, Nathanael said to his father, "Do you know the best part of the party?"

"The great food?"

"No," said Nathanael.

"The singing?"

"No. The best part of it all was that I became friends with Joshua next door. I never talked to him before because I thought he was blind and wouldn't be much fun. But he's really great. He invited me to come and play at his house tomorrow."

Nathanael's mother gave him a hug. "You had a wonderful bar mitzvah party," she said. "And now you also have a new friend."

God's shalom is a little like that party.

Moses Sees God

BASED ON EXODUS 33:12–23

Moses sometimes got very mixed up.

Moses wanted to understand God. He also wanted to understand the people of Israel. Sometimes he would just hold his head with his hands and feel very sad. "There are so many things I don't understand."

So Moses went to talk with God. "Please help me, God," said Moses. "I want to understand you."

"What would you like me to explain?" asked God.

"Well, I've seen the wonderful things you've done. I've seen how you got the people of Israel out of Egypt. I've seen how you brought us food, when we were hungry. I've seen how you got water from a rock, when we were thirsty. But…" Moses just stood there and shook his head.

"But what?" God's voice was soft and kind.

"I haven't seen *you.* I want to know what you look like. I want to see your face."

"That's a hard thing, Moses," said God. "It's very hard for people to see me. You can see what I do. You can feel my love in your heart. I am all around you just like the air is all around you. But you can't see me."

"But I want to see you," Moses was crying a little. "I want to see you, so I know who you are."

"Moses," said God. "You have worked very hard to help me. You have worked hard to help the people of Israel. So I am going to do something special for you."

"I can't let you see my face because, you see, I am not a human like you are. I don't have a head or legs or arms like you have. I'm not a man or a woman. I'm not old or young. I'm different than anything you know. But maybe I can show you something that will help you understand.

"Go to the big rock that you can see right in front of you. There's a crack right through the centre of it. Look through that crack. I'll show you something of who I am."

So Moses went to the big rock. He looked through the crack. For a while, it felt as if a kind, warm hand was covering his eyes.

Then the hand went away and Moses saw… He wasn't sure what he saw.

Moses tried to tell his sister, Miriam, about it. "It was like a flash of lightning, except it wasn't loud. It wasn't hard. It was as if my whole body was filled with light. It was as if I was filled with something good and strong."

"But what you saw was a light?" asked Miriam.

"What I saw was bright and beautiful. But that was only a small part of it, Miriam. Now I feel as if I really know God. And I know for sure that God will always be with me, and with all the people of Israel."

Trouble for Jesus

BASED ON MATTHEW 22:15–22

The people of Israel had to give money to the Roman emperor. He was like a very powerful king. He sent his soldiers to Israel. The soldiers said, "The emperor is your ruler now. You have to do what the emperor tells you. You have to give him money. If you don't, we will hurt you."

The people of Israel didn't like this. "Only God should tell us what to do. And God doesn't want us to give money to the Roman soldiers," they said. "That's a bad thing to do."

One day, some of the leaders of Israel wanted to make trouble for Jesus. "How can we make him say something that will get him into trouble?" they said.

"Let's ask him about giving money to the Roman emperor," said another.

"That's a good idea. We can trick Jesus. If he says we should give money to the emperor, then the people of Israel will be angry at him. If he says, no, we should not give money to the emperor, we should only give money to God, then the Roman soldiers will be angry. They'll grab him and they'll put him in jail."

So they went to find Jesus.

"Jesus," they said, "we know that you are a good person. We know that you live God's way, and that you want all of us to live God's way. So tell us, please, should we pay money to the Roman soldiers? Or should we give our money to God? What is the right thing to do?"

Jesus looked at the leaders of Israel and smiled. He knew they were trying to play a mean trick on him.

"When people pay money to the Roman emperor, how do they do that?" Jesus asked.

"They give some coins to his soldiers."

"Show me one of those coins," said Jesus.

One of the leaders of Israel dug down into his pocket. He found a coin and gave it to Jesus.

"Look at this. There's a picture on this coin," said Jesus. "Whose picture is it?"

"The emperor's!" said the leaders of Israel.

"Does that mean that the coin belongs to the emperor?"

"I suppose so," said one of the leaders.

"Well, then," said Jesus, "if it belongs to the emperor, give it to him. Do you belong to the emperor?" Jesus asked.

"No! No! We belong to God," replied the leaders.

"Then give yourselves to God," said Jesus. "Give God all your love and learn to live God's way."

The leaders of Israel didn't know what to say. They walked away very slowly. Then one of them whispered, "We tried to trick Jesus. But it didn't work. Let's go away and think of some other way to make trouble for him."

Moses Sees a New Land

BASED ON DEUTERONOMY 34

Moses stood on top of Mount Nebo. From there, he could see the land of Canaan. This was the land that God had promised to the Hebrew people.

Moses felt sad and happy. He was sad and happy as he thought about all the things that had happened in his life.

Moses remembered how God had spoken to him from a burning bush. God told Moses to lead the people out of Egypt. Moses remembered how God had kept them in the desert for 40 years.

The desert had been like a school. God had wanted the Hebrew people to know what it meant to be God's chosen people, God's special people. That's why God had given them the Ten Commandments and many other lessons about how to live in God's way.

Moses was sad. The Hebrew people had found it so hard to trust God. They found it hard to believe that God would be with them, even when bad things were

happening to them. But Moses was happy. Now, at last, the Hebrew people were ready to go into the land God had promised.

It looked like such a beautiful land, from there on top of Mount Nebo. That made Moses happy. It would be good for the Hebrew people to get out of the hot, dry desert. But Moses felt sad. God had said to Moses, "I will let you see this new land with your eyes, but you can't go into it."

Moses was 120 years old. He was still strong and healthy, but he knew he would die soon.

So Moses asked one of his helpers, Joshua, to stand beside him. "People of Israel," said Moses, "Joshua has God's spirit in him. I am going to die soon. God has asked Joshua to be your leader."

Then Moses put his hand on Joshua and said a prayer to God. "Please, God, help Joshua be a good leader. Help him to listen to all the things you say."

Not long after that, Moses died. The people of Israel were very sad.

Since then, the people of Israel have never had a leader like Moses. They all said it was because Moses was the only one who talked to God face to face.

The Most Important Things

BASED ON MATTHEW 22:34–40

Love God with all your heart, soul, and mind.

AND...

Love your neighbour.

Jesus went to many places telling people about God's love. "Be kind and fair to people," he said. "Be extra kind and fair to people who are poor, or who are hurt."

Some of the rulers of Israel didn't like that. "People should be listening to *us*, not to Jesus!" So the rulers would ask Jesus hard questions. They hoped Jesus would say something wrong. "If he doesn't give us the right answer, then we can make trouble for him!"

"We would like to ask you a question," they said one day.

"Good," said Jesus. "It's good to ask questions. That's how we learn."

"In all the stories and songs we have learned about God and about the people of Israel, what is the most important thing?"

"That's easy," said Jesus. "Love God. Love God with all your heart. Love God with all your soul. Love God with all your mind.

"And here is a second thing. It's almost the same as the first. Love your neighbour. Your neighbours are all the people you know – people who live near your home, people in your church. In your school. They are people all over the world."

Jesus smiled at the rulers again. "If you can remember these two things – love God and love your neighbour – then you know the most important things about how to live God's way."

The People Claim the Promised Land

BASED ON JOSHUA 1, 3 – 4

Joshua was a little bit afraid. He didn't know if he could be as good a leader as Moses.

But God said to Joshua, "Don't be afraid. I will help you feel strong. I want you to lead the people into the Promised Land so that my promise to Abraham and Sarah can come true. I will be with you wherever you go."

So Joshua led all the Hebrew people out of the desert and into a land called Canaan. It had been a long journey through the desert from Egypt. Now, at last, the Hebrew people were in the land God had promised to them.

To get into Canaan, the people had to cross the river Jordan. "How will we get across?" they wondered. But as soon as their feet touched the water, the river got dry.

Everyone was surprised. "God did this for us," said Joshua. "God has helped us again. We must do something to remember this."

The Hebrew people were divided into 12 very large families. These families had aunts and uncles and cousins and second cousins. These big families were called "tribes." Sometimes there were hundreds of people in a tribe.

"Let the leader of each tribe find a big stone from the middle of the river. Bring each stone up to the other side of the river. From now on, whenever people see these stones, they will remember what God has done for us."

When the Hebrew people had all crossed the river, the water started flowing again.

So they said "thank you" to God in a very special way. They had a Passover meal, with some special food. It was their first meal with food from the new country, Canaan. The Hebrew people remembered how God had brought them out of Egypt. They remembered the promise God had made to Abraham and Sarah.

"Thank you, God," said Joshua. "You got us out of Egypt. You took care of us in the desert. Now we are in a new country. We're not slaves anymore. We are free."

Jesus Turns Things Upside Down

BASED ON MATTHEW 23:11–12

Mary and Peter and Jesus and all their friends went to the synagogue. They did this every Sabbath.

A synagogue is like a church. Jesus and his friends went there to pray to God and to sing songs about God.

They also went to the synagogue to see many of their other friends. When the praying and singing were done, all the people would gather to have something good to eat and to drink. And they would stand around and talk.

One day, after synagogue, Peter and Mary began to talk about the people they met there. "Who is the most important person here?" Peter wondered.

"It could be the rabbi – the teacher," said Mary. "Or maybe the person who leads the singing."

"I know what Jesus would say," said Peter. "He always turns things upside down."

"You're right," laughed Mary. "He would tell us that the smallest child, sitting at the very back of the synagogue, would be the most important person."

"Jesus told us once that if you think you are the most important person, you are really the opposite. You are not important at all. And if you think you are not important, then you really are the most important one of all."

Mary laughed again. "I remember when he told us that the most important person is the one who is the servant – the one who helps other people."

"And look over there," said Peter. He pointed to the other side of the synagogue. "There's Jesus taking a plate of food and some juice to that old lady. She was sitting right at the very back when we were singing and praying. She couldn't even stand up to sing."

"Jesus is showing her that she's important," said Mary. "Jesus really likes to turn things upside down. The last one will be first, and the first one will be last."

The People of Israel Remember

BASED ON JOSHUA 24:24–29

Bit by bit, the Hebrew people – the people of Israel – began to live in many parts of Canaan. It was a nice place. They believed God had given it to them. But the land of Canaan wasn't empty. There were people living there already.

Some of the people who lived in Canaan came and said to the people of Israel, "We live very far away. And we are very poor. Promise you won't attack us."

"We promise," said the Hebrews.

Then the people of Israel found out these people didn't live far away, and they were not poor. So the Hebrews said, "You tricked us!"

"Yes," said the people of Canaan, "but you promised not to attack us."

"We won't attack you," said the Hebrew people, "but because you tricked us, you have to carry our water and get wood for our fires. You have to work for us. You will have to be like slaves to us."

The people of Israel had already forgotten how awful it was to be slaves. Sometimes they forgot how God had brought them out of Egypt, where they had been slaves.

More and more, the people of Israel began to find places to live in the land of Canaan. Joshua was still their leader, but he was getting very old. He

wondered if the people of Israel would remember to live in God's way.

Joshua asked all the people to come together in one place. He set a big rock up on its end and said, "This rock will remind us how to live in God's way. It will remind our children. And our children's children."

Then Joshua said to the people of Israel, "Remember the promise God made to Abraham and Sarah. God has kept that promise, and now we have a land of our own to live in. Now we must keep our part of the promise."

Then the people said to Joshua, "We will remember to live in God's way."

"Are you sure?" asked Joshua.

"Yes," said the people. "We will try our very best."

Soon after that Joshua died. The people were very sad. Joshua had been a good leader.

Amos, the Farmer Prophet

BASED ON AMOS, SELECTED VERSES

Amos didn't really plan to be a prophet. A prophet is someone who helps people understand how to live God's way. Amos knew how to take care of sheep. He knew how to grow nice fruit on fig trees.

It surprised Amos when God asked him to be a prophet. "I'm a farmer," Amos said to God. "But if that's what you want me to do, I'll do it."

So Amos looked around. He saw how the poor people had hardly anything to eat. They had no place to live. Amos also saw that rich people lived in very big houses. They ate too much and got fat. Often they got rich by cheating the poor people.

Amos noticed that many people were slaves. A slave is a person who belongs to someone else. Like a horse or a dog. If you were a slave, your owner could hit you or even kill you.

Then Amos knew what God wanted him to say.

"Listen to God," said Amos. "These people sell other people for money. The poor slaves get sold for the price of a pair of shoes. The rich walk all over the poor, the way they walk on the ground. If you don't stop treating people this way, God will punish you."

Of course, people hardly ever listened to the prophets. They didn't want to hear what God was telling them.

Amos kept trying.

"Listen to God's words," Amos said. "'I hate it when you get together and have a big feast. I can't stand the fancy meetings you have. I hate the songs you sing. They are like noise to me. I won't listen to them.

'This is what I want. I want justice. I want justice, where everybody is fair to everyone else. I don't want you to hurt other people or take things away from them. I want you to be kind to everyone.

'I want justice to roll like a river.

'I want your goodness to run

like a stream that never stops.'"

When the people heard that, they talked to their king. "We don't like the things Amos is saying. We want to keep our big houses. We want to keep our slaves. Tell Amos to stop saying those things."

"I'll do even better," said the king. "I'll send Amos back to where he came from – back to his sheep and his fig trees."

Amos was sad when the king told him to stop being a prophet. He went back to his home. But even in his home Amos kept trying to help people grow in God's way.

The Wedding Party

BASED ON MATTHEW 25:1–13

Jesus told many stories about God's shalom. Each story helps us to understand a little more of what Jesus meant. In this story, Jesus says that God's shalom is a little bit like a big party after a wedding. But if you want to come to the party, you have to get ready. Now.

Abigail and Isaac had decided to get married. They loved each other very much.

"We want everyone in our village to come to our wedding. It's going to be a really big party. We don't have enough money to buy food for everyone at the party, but if each person brings a little food, there will be enough."

"When is your wedding going to be?" asked the people of the village.

"We don't know, exactly," said Abigail. "Isaac and I have to go to another village because of our work. When we both get back home, we'll have the wedding. So get ready. Now."

Some of the people in the village began to get food ready right away. "We want to have it all prepared so that as soon as Abigail and Isaac come home, we can have the wedding."

But some of the other people in the village didn't get ready. "There's lots of time for that," they said.

Then, one day, they heard someone running down the

street yelling, "Abigail and Isaac are coming. Grab your food and come! Let's start the wedding party!"

All those people who had their food ready ran to the wedding party. They began to sing and to dance and to share all the great food.

The people who didn't get any food ready ran to their houses. "We have to cook something fast. Hurry!" Finally, they had their food cooked. They put the food into baskets and began to run to the wedding. "We hope we're not too late!" they said.

Coming down the street they saw the people who had gone to the wedding. "The party is all over," they said. "You missed Abigail and Isaac's wedding because you weren't ready. Too bad! The party was such fun."

A Mother for Israel

BASED ON JUDGES 4 – 5

The people of Israel began to live all over the land of Canaan. Usually they called themselves "Hebrews." They remembered the story of God's promise; God's covenant. They remembered what happened to Jacob. Then they called themselves "the people of Israel."

But often they forgot the story. The people of Israel forgot the promise they had made to God when Joshua died.

Many other people lived in Canaan, too. Sometimes one group of people tried to be the boss over other groups, and then there would be fighting. Many people were hurt or killed.

Most of the people who lived in Canaan had kings and queens to tell them what to do. But not the people of Israel.

Whenever the people of Israel were in trouble, God would send a leader to help them. They called these leaders "judges." These leaders weren't like judges who sat in a court. They were leaders who helped the Hebrew people when there was an argument about something. Sometimes they were prophets. Prophets are people who love God very much and help others understand what God wants them to do. Sometimes the judges were like generals of an army. One of the strongest and best judges was Deborah.

The people of Israel were in trouble. They had been fighting with the king of Canaan. They lost the fight. Now the king of Canaan was hurting them.

Deborah was a prophet. She was a strong, wise leader who helped people understand how to live in God's way.

When one of the people of Israel was having an argument with another Hebrew person, they would both come to Deborah. "Please help us decide what to do."

Many of the Hebrew people came to Deborah to tell her about the cruel things the king of Canaan was doing. Finally, Deborah said, "We will get some people together and fight the king of Canaan."

Deborah thought that Barak would be a good leader for the army. So she sent him a letter and said, "Please come to see me."

When Barak came to Deborah, she said, "Get 10,000 people together. Go and fight the king of Canaan."

Barak said to her, "I'm afraid to go by myself. If you go with me, I will go to fight the king."

The people of Israel who were going to fight the king were afraid. Deborah helped them to feel brave and strong. "Deborah is our leader. She is like a strong mother in Israel," the people said. "She helps us feel we can do important things."

Barak and the people of Israel were able to beat the king of Canaan, and so they were free again.

Then Deborah and Barak sang a song together. Some of the words went like this:

> We had terrible days in our country,
> a very hard time in our land.
> In the small towns, nothing could happen,
> no one could travel the roads.
> A strong mother arose in Israel,
> a leader whose name was Deborah.
> Deborah helped us remember,
> remember the promise of God.

An Upside Down Story

BASED ON MATTHEW 25:14–30

Jesus liked to teach people by telling them stories. We call those stories parables.

Sometimes Jesus would make up funny stories that seemed to turn everything upside down.

One day Jesus told his friends a really strange story.

There was a very rich man who wanted to go on a trip. "I need someone to take care of my money," he said to himself. So he called his servants.

"Here," he said to the first servant. "Here are five bags of money. Take care of them until I get back home."

Then the rich man called the second servant. "Here are two bags of money," he said. "Take care of them till I get back home."

The rich man still had some money left over, so he called another servant. "Here is one bag of money. Take care of it till I get back home."

And so the rich man went on his trip. The first servant took his five bags of money and bought a gold mine. The second servant took his two bags of money and bought an oil well.

The third servant took his one bag of money and hid it safely in the ground.

A whole year later, the rich man came back home. He called his three servants. "I have been away for a long time," he said. "Tell me what you have done with my money."

The first servant came up and gave the rich man ten bags of money. "Wow!" said the rich man. "Where did you get all that money?"

"I bought a gold mine with your five bags of money. I got a lot of gold out of that mine, and so now you have ten bags of money."

"That's great!" said the rich man. "Because you did so well with the five bags of money, I am going to give you a whole lot more money, and you can see what you can do with it."

Then the second servant came and gave the rich man five bags of money. "I took your two bags of money and I bought an oil well. The oil well gave me lots of oil to sell, so that now you have five bags of money."

"That's great!" said the rich man. "Because you did so well with the two bags of money, I am going to give you a whole lot more money, and you can see what you can do with it."

Then the rich man asked the third servant, "I gave you one bag of money. What did you do with it?"

The third servant looked up at the rich man. "I knew that you are the kind of man who takes things that don't belong to him. I knew that you often take money away from poor people. So I took your money and I buried it in the ground. Here is your bag of money."

"What?" yelled the rich man. "I gave you one bag of money and all you do is give the same bag of money back to me? Why didn't you do something with it so I would have more money?"

The third servant was very afraid. "But I did what you asked me to do."

"Get out of here!" the rich man yelled. "I don't ever want to see you again. You can go work for somebody else. Give me my money and just get out of here!"

And that's the way it is. The rich people get richer, and the poor people get poorer.

When Jesus had finished telling his story he smiled at his friends. They all looked worried.

"Did you like my story?" he asked.

"No, I didn't like your story," said Andrew. "The third servant did the right thing. And it isn't fair that rich people keep getting more money, and the poor people keep getting poorer."

"Andrew," said Jesus. "I'm glad you didn't like my story. I didn't like it either."

"I get it," said Mary. "You were joking with us again," Jesus. "You were turning things upside down."

"Yes! That's right, Mary," said Jesus. "I told you a story about the way things are. The poor people who try to do the right thing, who try to live in God's way, often become even poorer. The rich people, who already have far more than they need, often take things away from the poor.

"So my story is about the way things are," said Jesus. "But that's not the way they should be. The third servant did the right thing, even though the rich man was very unkind and very unfair. The third servant was living God's way!"

PROPER 29 [34]

(REIGN OF CHRIST)

Being Kind to God

BASED ON MATTHEW 25:31 – 40

Jesus liked to talk about "the kingdom of heaven."

But his friends didn't always understand what he meant. "Does this mean there is going to be a king with a crown?" asked Mary of Magdala. "Will this king ride a white horse or sit on a golden throne?"

Jesus smiled. "No, Mary," said Jesus. "It's not like any kingdom you know about. Can I tell you a parable?"

"Sure," said Mary. She liked Jesus' stories.

"Close your eyes and pretend you can see this kingdom," said Jesus. "Pretend you can see a very kind king. Or a queen. Whichever you like.

"Now this ruler – this queen or king – has all the people gathered around. 'I want all the good people – all the people who have tried to live God's way – I would like them to come and live with me forever,' said the ruler.

"'How will we know which people tried to live God's way?' they asked.

"'This is how you will know,' said the ruler. 'When I was hungry, you gave me something to eat. When I was thirsty, you gave me a drink. When I felt lonely, you came to be with me. When I was cold, you gave me some of your clothes. When I was sick, you cared for me. When I was in jail, you came to see me.'

"'But how can that be?' said the people. 'We don't remember giving you anything to eat or wear. You are the ruler, so you don't need those things from us. When did we do kind things for you?'

"'You did many kind things for me,' said the ruler. 'When you were kind to one of the homeless people on the street, you were being kind to me. When you gave some money to help poor people, that was the same as giving it to me.

"'You see, all those people you were kind to are part of my family. When you help the poorest and weakest ones in my family, you are helping me.'"

Mary of Magdala smiled. "I understand now. That queen or king in the story is God. And everyone is part of God's family. So when we are kind and try to help each other, we are helping someone in God's family. We are really being kind to God."

ALL SAINTS DAY

Singing for God

A PARAPHRASE OF SOME VERSES FROM PSALM 34

Note to leaders: *Today's gospel reading, Matthew 5:1–12, is also the reading for the Fourth Sunday after Epiphany. The story "Jesus Teaches," which goes with this text, can be found on page 58.*

All the time I'll sing to God;
I'll sing my song to God.
God is always good to me,
so I'll be good to God's world.

I tasted some honey. It tasted like God,
'cause God is so sweet and so good.
I tasted fresh bread. It tasted like God,
'cause God helps me be big and strong.

When I think about God, I am almost afraid,
and yet I'm not scared at all.
When I sing about God, I shake just a little,
yet I laugh and I sing really loud.

Whenever I cry, I know God hears.
I'm sure God's sad when I hurt.
Whenever I laugh, I know God smiles.
God smiles with me when I'm happy.

All the time I'll sing to God;
I'll sing my song to God.
God has always been good to me,
so I'll be good to God's world.

The Whole Earth Says Thanks

A PARAPHRASE OF SOME VERSES FROM PSALM 65

Dear God, I love to sing to you,
because you sing back to me.
When bad things happen and I feel sad,
you sing to me in my heart.

Dear God, you made the mountains so tall,
you made the ocean so blue,
and yet, you are stronger than all of them,
strong, and kind and true.

Dear God, you always give us rain,
and sun for the plants to grow.
You give us food and you give us friends;
we couldn't ask you for more.

Dear God, you gave us the bright green forest,
you gave us the hills and the flowers.
You gave us the skies and the lakes and the streams,
and the whole earth shouts and says thanks.

THANKSGIVING

Saying "Thank You" to God

BASED ON LUKE 17:11–19

Jesus was walking all the way to the city of Jerusalem. It was a long walk from his home in Nazareth. It took several days.

As Jesus was walking, a group of ten people came up to him. These people had leprosy. Leprosy is a skin disease.

In Jesus' day, people were very afraid of leprosy. If someone got this disease, they wouldn't be able to live in their home anymore. "Go away," their family and friends would say. "Go live by yourself. We don't want to catch your skin disease."

The ten people with leprosy came to Jesus. "Please help us," they said. "We are very sick. Can you help us get better? Please, Jesus! Please!"

Jesus felt very sad for them. "Yes, I can help you," he said. "Go to the temple and show yourselves to the priests."

So the ten people went as fast as they could to do what Jesus had told them.

But one of the people stopped and came back to Jesus. "Thank you so much, Jesus," he said. "Thank you!"

"There were ten people who had leprosy who asked me for help," said Jesus. "Where are the others? Don't they want to say thank you to God?"

"I don't know where they are," said the man.

"Well, you are here to thank God," said Jesus. "I can tell that you are someone who tries to live God's way. Go back to your family and friends. Remind them to say thank you to God."

MOVEMENTS TO "A SONG FROM THE BIBLE" ON PAGE 123

The movements to this psalm were suggested by Keri Wehlander, poet, lyricist, and liturgical dancer. Practise until you can do all these motions in one fluid dance. If working with children take the time to teach the actions slowly until each step is mastered.

1.

God, you are wonderful. When I think of your love, I feel strong... *(Start with one knee on the ground and gradually stretch arms above head.)*

2.

You have made the stars in the sky... *(Stand and stretch out arms and lift head.)*

3.

and you made me – a tiny new baby... *(Bring arms into chest as if holding a baby.)*

4.

Oh, God, when I look up at the sky, at the moon and the stars that you made... *(Spin around with arms spread wide.)*

5.

I feel so small, so tiny and weak... *(Crunch down onto knees and cover face with hands.)*

6.

Do you care about children?... *(Move arms to one side underneath bowed head and stretch arm above head with hand bent back.)*

7.

Do you care about grown-ups, too?... *(Stretch both arms upward and look up while moving to kneeling position.)*

8.

You made us, God, to be a little like you. Because of that, we are strong and loving... *(Move to standing and place hands on heart.)*

9.

You've given us the world to take care of, all the animals and all the birds, and everything else in the world... *(Bend down and create a scooping action as if to scoop up all the world.)*

10.

God, you are wonderful. When I think of your love, I feel strong... *(Repeat step 2 – stand and stretch out arms and lift head.)*

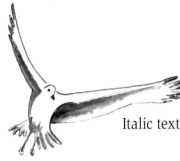

Lectionary Index
Italic text indicates stories included in this volume.

Advent 1..13
Isaiah 2:1–5
Psalm 122
Romans 13:11–14
Matthew 24:36–44

Advent 2..21
Isaiah 11:1–10
Psalm 72:1-7, 18-19
Romans 15:4-13
Matthew 3:1–12

Advent 3..27
Isaiah 35:1–10
Psalm 146:5-10 or Luke 1:47-55
James 5:7-10
Matthew 11:2–11

Advent 4..33
Isaiah 7:10–16
Psalm 80:1-7, 17-19
Romans 1:1-7
Matthew 1:18–25

Christmas Day, Proper 3................................37
Isaiah 52:7-10
Psalm 98
Hebrews 1:1-4, (5-12)
John 1:1–14

First Sunday after Christmas................................38
Isaiah 63:7-9
Psalm 148
Hebrews 2:10-18
Matthew 2:13–23

Epiphany..42
Isaiah 60:1-6
Psalm 72:1-7, 10-14
Ephesians 3:1-12
Matthew 2:1–12

Baptism of Jesus..44
First Sunday after Epiphany
Isaiah 42:1-9
Psalm 29
Acts 10:34–43
Matthew 3:13–17

Second Sunday after Epiphany................................48
Isaiah 49:1-7
Psalm 40:1-11
1 Corinthians 1:1–9
John 1:29–42

Third Sunday after Epiphany................................52
Isaiah 9:1–4
Psalm 27:1, 4-9
1 Corinthians 1:10-18
Matthew 4:12–23

Fourth Sunday after Epiphany................................57
Micah 6:1–8
Psalm 15
1 Corinthians 1:18-31
Matthew 5:1–12

Fifth Sunday after Epiphany................................60
Isaiah 58:1-9a, (9b-12)
Psalm 112:1-9, (10)
1 Corinthians 2:1–12, (13–16)
Matthew 5:13–20

Sixth Sunday after Epiphany................................63
Deuteronomy 30:15-20 or Sirach 15:15-20
Psalm 119:1-8
1 Corinthians 3:1-9
Matthew 5:21–37

Seventh Sunday after Epiphany................................64
Leviticus 19:1-2, 9-18
Psalm 119:33-40
1 Corinthians 3:10–11, 16–23
Matthew 5:38–48

Eighth Sunday after Epiphany................................67
Isaiah 49:8–16a
Psalm 131
1 Corinthians 4:1-5
Matthew 6:24–34

Ninth Sunday after Epiphany................................70
Deuteronomy 11:18-21, 26-28
Psalm 31:1-5, 19-24
Romans 1:16-17; 3:22b-28, (29-31)
Matthew 7:21–29

Transfiguration Sunday................................72
Exodus 24:12–18
Psalm 2 or Psalm 99
2 Peter 1:16-21
Matthew 17:1–9

Lent 1..76
Genesis 2:15–17; 3:1–7
Psalm 32
Romans 5:12-19
Matthew 4:1–11

Lent 2 80
Genesis 12:1–4a
Psalm 121
Romans 4:1–5, 13–17
John 3:1–17 or Matthew 17:1–9

Lent 3 84
Exodus 17:1–7
Psalm 95
Romans 5:1–11
John 4:5–42

Lent 4 87
1 Samuel 16:1–13
Psalm 23
Ephesians 5:8–14
John 9:1–41

Lent 5 89
Ezekiel 37:1–14
Psalm 130
Romans 8:6–11
John 11:1–45

Passion/Palm Sunday 91
Liturgy of the Palms
    Matthew 21:1–11
    Psalm 118:1–2, 19–29
Liturgy of the Passion
    Isaiah 50:4–9a
    Psalm 31:9–16
    Philippians 2:5–11
    Matthew 26:14 – 27:66 or Matthew 27:11–54

Easter 98
1st reading
    Acts 10:34–43 or Jeremiah 31:1–6
    Psalm 118:1–2, 14–24
2nd reading
    Colossians 3:1–4 or Acts 10:34–43
    Gospel
    John 20:1–18 or Matthew 28:1–10

Second Sunday of Easter 100
Acts 2:14a, 22–32
Psalm 16
1 Peter 1:3–9
John 20:19–31

Third Sunday of Easter 102
Acts 2:14a, 36–41
Psalm 116:1–4, 12–19
1 Peter 1:17–23
Luke 24:13–35

Fourth Sunday of Easter 105
Acts 2:42–47
Psalm 23
1 Peter 2:19–25
John 10:1–10

Fifth Sunday of Easter 108
Acts 7:55–60
Psalm 31:1–5, 15–16
1 Peter 2:2–10
John 14:1–14

Sixth Sunday of Easter 112
Acts 17:22–31
Psalm 66:8–20
1 Peter 3:13–22
John 14:15–21

Seventh Sunday of Easter 114
Acts 1:6–14
Psalm 68:1–10, 32–35
1 Peter 4:12–14; 5:6–11
John 17:1–11

Pentecost 116
1st reading
    Acts 2:1–21 or Numbers 11:24–30
    Psalm 104:24–34, 35b
2nd reading
    1 Corinthians 12:3b–13 or Acts 2:1–21
Gospel
    John 20:19–23 or John 7:37–39

Trinity Sunday (First Sunday after Pentecost) 121
Genesis 1:1 – 2:4a
Psalm 8
2 Corinthians 13:11–13
Matthew 28:16–20

Proper 4 [9] 124
Sunday between May 29 and June 4 inclusive
Genesis 6:9–22; 7:24; 8:14–19 | Deuteronomy 11:18–21, 26–28
Psalm 46 | Psalm 31:1–5, 19–24
            Romans 1:16–17; 3:22b–28, (29–31)
            Matthew 7:21–29

Proper 5 [10] 128
Sunday between June 5 and June 11 inclusive
Genesis 12:1–9 | Hosea 5:15 – 6:6
Psalm 33:1–12 | Psalm 50:7–15
            Romans 4:13–25
            Matthew 9:9–13, 18–26

Proper 6 [11] 133
Sunday between June 12 and June 18 inclusive
Genesis 18:1–15, (21:1–7) | Exodus 19:2–8a
Psalm 116:1–2, 12–19 | Psalm 100
            Romans 5:1–8
            Matthew 9:35 – 10:8, (9–23)

Proper 7 [12] 139
Sunday between June 19 and June 25 inclusive
Genesis 21:8–21 | Jeremiah 20:7–13
Psalm 86:1–10, 16–17 | Psalm 69:7–10, (11–15), 16–18
            Romans 6:1b–11
            Matthew 10:24–39

Proper 8 [13] 142
Sunday between June 26 and July 2 inclusive
Genesis 22:1–14 | Jeremiah 28:5–9
Psalm 13 | Psalm 89:1–4, 15–18
            Romans 6:12–23
            Matthew 10:40–42

Proper 9 [14] 147
Sunday between July 3 and July 9 inclusive
Genesis 24:34–38, 42–49, 58–67 | Zechariah 9:9–12
Psalm 45:10–17 | Psalm 145:8–14
   or Song of Solomon 2:8–13
            Romans 7:15–25a
            Matthew 11:16–19, 25–30

Proper 10 [15] 152
Sunday between July 10 and July 16 inclusive
Genesis 25:19–34 | Isaiah 55:10–13
Psalm 119:105–112 | Psalm 65:(1–8), 9–13
            Romans 8:1–11
            Matthew 13:1–9, 18–23

Proper 11 [16] 156
Sunday between July 17 and July 23 inclusive
Genesis 28:10–19a | Wisdom of Solomon 12:13, 16–19
                        or Isaiah 44:6–8
Psalm 139:1–12, 23–24 | Psalm 86:11–17
            Romans 8:12–25
            Matthew 13:24–30, 36–43

Proper 12 [17] 164
Sunday between July 24 and July 30 inclusive
Genesis 29:15–28 | 1 Kings 3:5–12
Palm 105:1–11, 45b | Psalm 119:129–136
   or Psalm 128
            Romans 8:26–39
            Matthew 13:31–33, 44–52

Proper 13 [18] 168
Sunday between July 31 and August 6 inclusive
Genesis 32:22–31 | Isaiah 55:1–5
Psalm 17:1–7, 15 | Psalm 145:8–9, 14–21
            Romans 9:1–5
            Matthew 14:13–21

Proper 14 [19] 174
Sunday between August 7 and August 13 inclusive
Genesis 37:1–4, 12–28 | 1 Kings 19:9–18
Psalm 105:1–6, 16–22, 45b | Psalm 85:8–13
            Romans 10:5–15
            Matthew 14:22–33

Proper 15 [20] 181
Sunday between August 14 and August 20 inclusive
Genesis 45:1–15 | Isaiah 56:1, 6–8
Psalm 133 | Psalm 67
         Romans 11:1–2a, 29–32
         Matthew 15:(10–20), 21–28

Proper 16 [21] 186
Sunday between August 21 and August 27 inclusive
Exodus 1:8 – 2:10 | Isaiah 51:1–6
Psalm 124 | Psalm 138
            Romans 12:1–8
            Matthew 16:13–20

Proper 17 [22] 191
Sunday between August 28 and September 3 inclusive
Exodus 3:1–15 | Jeremiah 15:15–21
Psalm 105:1–6, 23–26, 45c | Psalm 26:1–8
            Romans 12:9–21
            Matthew 16:21–28

Proper 18 [23] 198
Sunday between September 4 and September 10 inclusive
Exodus 12:1–14 | Ezekiel 33:7–11
Psalm 149 | Psalm 119:33–40
            Romans 13:8–14
            Matthew 18:15–20

Proper 19 [24] 203
Sunday between September 11 and September 17 inclusive
Exodus 14:19–31 | Genesis 50:15–21
Psalm 114 | Psalm 103:(1–7), 8–13
   or Exodus 15:16–11, 20–21
            Romans 14:1–12
            Matthew 18:21–35

Proper 20 [25] 206
Sunday between September 18 and September 24 inclusive
Exodus 16:2–15 | Jonah 3:10 – 4:11
Psalm 105:1–6, 37–45 | Psalm 145:1–8
            Philippians 1:21–30
            Matthew 20:1–16

Proper 21 [26] 209
Sunday between September 25 and October 1 inclusive
Exodus 17:1–7 | Ezekiel 18:1–4, 25–32
Psalm 78:1–4, 12–16 | Psalm 25:1–9
            Philippians 2:1–13
            Matthew 21:23–32

Proper 22 [27] 213
Sunday between October 2 and October 8 inclusive
Exodus 20:1–4, 7–9, 12–20 | Isaiah 5:1–7
Psalm 19 | Psalm 80:7–15
            Philippians 3:4b–14
            Matthew 21:33–46

Proper 23 [28] 218
Sunday between October 9 and October 15 inclusive
Exodus 32:1–14 | Isaiah 25:1–9
Psalm 106:1–6, 19–23 | Psalm 23
            Philippians 4:1–9
            Matthew 22:1–14

Proper 24 [29] 222
Sunday between October 16 and October 22 inclusive
Exodus 33:12–23 | Isaiah 45:1–7
Psalm 99 | Psalm 96:1–9, (10–13)
            1 Thessalonians 1:1–10
            Matthew 22:15–22

Proper 25 [30] 226
Sunday between October 23 and October 29 inclusive
Deuteronomy 34:1–12 | Leviticus 19:1–2, 15–18
Psalm 90:1–6, 13–17 | Psalm 1
     1 Thessalonians 2:1–8
     Matthew 22:34–46

Proper 26 [31]....................................229
Sunday between October 30 and November 5 inclusive
Joshua 3:7–17 | Micah 3:5–12
Psalm 107:1–7, 33–37 | Psalm 43
     1 Thessalonians 2:9–13
     Matthew 23:1–12

Proper 27 [32] 232
Sunday between November 6 and November 12 inclusive
Joshua 24:1–3a, 14–25 | Wisdom of Solomon 6:12–16
     or *Amos 5:18–24*
Psalm 78:1–7 | Wisdom of Solomon 6:17–20
     or Psalm 70
     1 Thessalonians 4:13–18
     Matthew 25:1–13

Proper 28 [33] 238
Sunday between November 13 and November 19
inclusive
Judges 4:1–7 | Zephaniah 1:7, 12–18
Psalm 123 | Psalm 90:1–8, (9–11), 12
     1 Thessalonians 5:1–11
     Matthew 25:14–30

Proper 29 [34] 242
(Reign of Christ or Christ the King)
Sunday between November 20 and November 26
inclusive
Ezekiel 34:11–16, 20–24 | Ezekiel 34:11–16, 20–24
Psalm 100 | Psalm 95:1–7a
     Ephesians 1:15–23
     Matthew 25:31–46

All Saints 244
November 1 or the first Sunday in November
Revelation 7:9–17
Psalm 34:1–10, 22
1 John 3:1–3
Matthew 5:1–12

Thanksgiving Day 246
Fourth Sunday in November (U.S.)
     or Second Monday in October (Canada)
Deuteronomy 8:7–18
Psalm 65
2 Corinthians 9:6–15
Luke 17:11–19

Dr. RALPH MILTON is a gifted story-teller, and the author of 17 books, including the bestselling *Family Story Bible; Angels in Red Suspenders;* and *Julian's Cell*, a novel based on the life of Julian of Norwich. On the Internet, Ralph Milton publishes the popular e-zine Rumors, which uses liberal doses of humour and story to communicate a lively faith. Co-founder of Wood Lake Publishing, Ralph Milton lives in Kelowna, British Columbia, with his wife and friend of 50 years, Beverley, a retired church minister. Together, they remain the ever-proud grandparents of Zoë and Jake.

MARGARET KYLE has been a part of the creative process at Wood Lake Publishing for 20 years. She has illus-trated many children's books includ-ing the bestselling, *Family Story Bible, by Ralph Milton* (1996) and *After the Beginning, by Carolyn Pogue* (2006). Margaret's artwork graces the cover of the new hymnal supplement, *More Voices.* (2007)

She lives in Okanagan Centre, British Columbia, with her husband, Michael Schwartzentruber.